# DORSET
## A PICTORIAL JOURNEY

**STEVE VIDLER**
TEXT BY DIANA LEPPARD

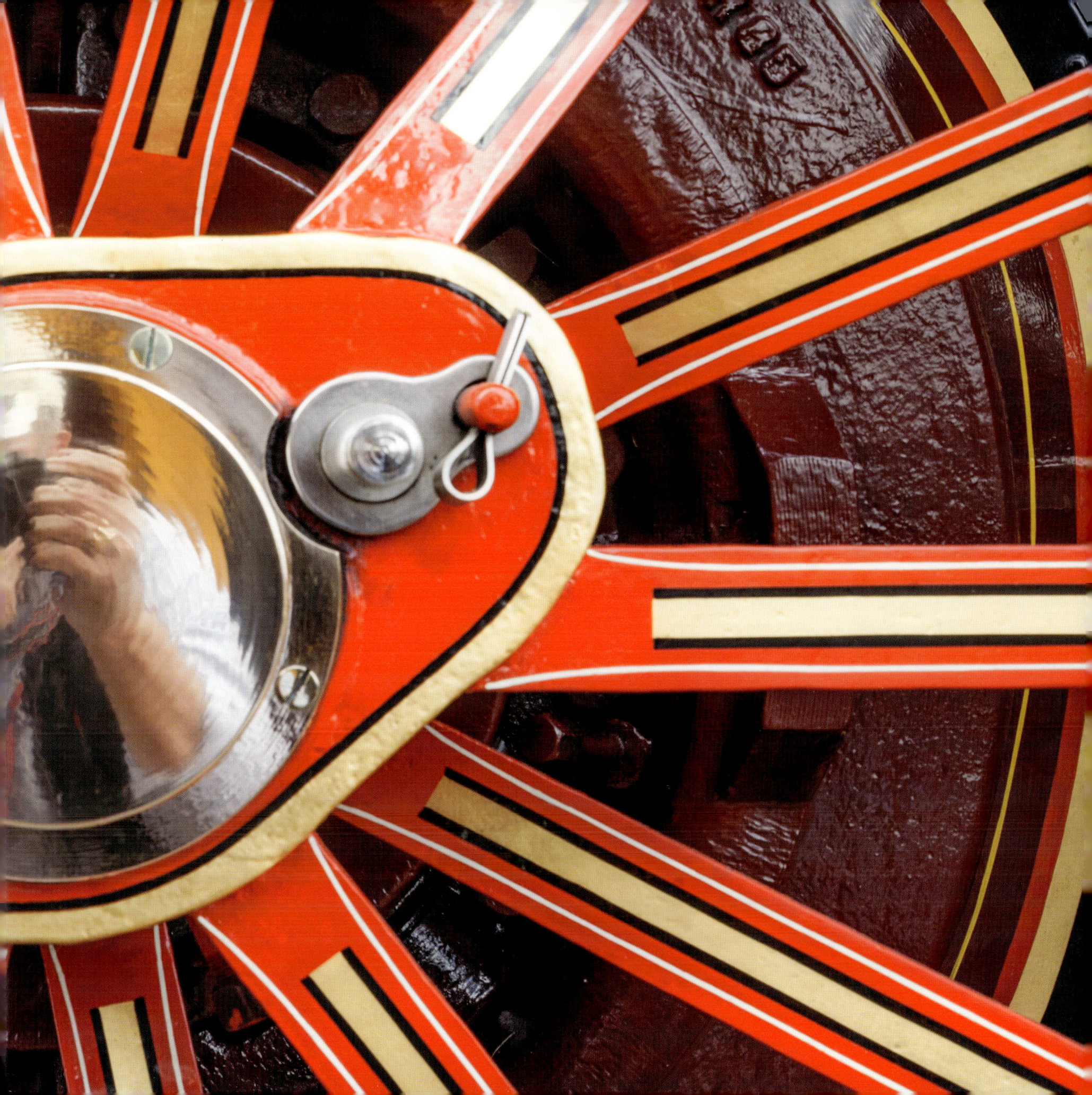

Published by Heartwood Publishing
Bath, United Kingdom
www.heartwoodpublishing.co.uk

Photography by Steve Vidler

Text by Diana Leppard

Book design by Ian Gordon, Artstyle

Photographs and text © Steve Vidler 2023

Except p.40 © Derek Davies

p.76 & p.102 © David John

p.148 © Alan Copson/AWL Images

Map © Anna Thompson 2023

All rights reserved. This book is sold subject to the condition that it shall not, by way of trade or otherwise, be lent, resold, hired out or otherwise circulated without Steve Vidler's prior written consent in any form of binding or cover other than that in which it is published and without a similar condition including this condition being imposed on the subsequent purchaser. No part of this publication may be reproduced, stored in a retrieval system or transmitted in any form or by any means, electronic and mechanical, photocopying, recording or otherwise without prior permission of Steve Vidler.

British Library Cataloguing in Publication Data

A catalogue record for this book is available from the British Library.

ISBN 978 1 914515 61 3

Printed and bound in India by
Replika Press Pvt Ltd

# DORSET

## A PICTORIAL JOURNEY

**MORE THAN SAND & SUNSHINE**
Bournemouth, Christchurch and Poole — 16

**THE PRETTY PENINSULA**
Around the Isle of Purbeck — 76

**THE TAIL OF WESSEX**
Dorchester, Weymouth and Portland Bill — 124

**A JURASSIC JAUNT**
Bridport, West Bay and Lyme Regis — 174

**FAR FROM THE MADDING CROWD**
Inland from West to East — 202

# DORSET

# MORE THAN SAND & SUNSHINE

The county of Dorset sits in a prime location between Hampshire and Devon on the sunny South Coast of England and attracts millions of visitors each year who come to enjoy some of the country's most beautiful scenery and fascinating heritage. Evidence of human settlement reaches back to Neolithic times and every individual who has since stepped on the land, from Alfred the Great to Thomas Hardy and J R R Tolkien, played a part in shaping the regional character seen today.

In 1974, the county boundary changed and the towns of Bournemouth, Poole and Christchurch, which were previously in Hampshire, became part of Dorset. These towns, which sit side-by-side in the south-east corner of the county, form the busiest area by far. Dorset has a population of just under 780,000 with more than half living around this ten-mile stretch of coastline.

The local population around Bournemouth is swollen by the millions of visitors who travel down to soak up the sun, eat ice cream and relax on the golden sand. Estimates of the average number of ice creams bought on the seven-mile seafront each year reach the heady heights of 750,000, with more than 20,000 eaten on a busy summer weekend. There are also around 3,500 traditional wooden deckchairs available to hire, whose canvas stripes add a colourful feel to the holiday atmosphere.

In 2011, Bournemouth beach was the scene of a successful World Record attempt, when 152 men and women donned their bathing gear on a chilly day and created a new record for the most people to take a shower simultaneously at a single venue. Unfortunately, this record has now been beaten by a group from Delaware in the USA, but the gauntlet is there to be taken up again.

Dorset is one of the most geologically interesting counties in England and the underlying rocks are key to the landscapes above. The geology of the south-east corner is younger than much of the county and is formed mainly of sand and clays, which support a heathland environment. There are a number of sites that have been designated as being of special scientific interest, including Hengistbury Head at the mouth of Christchurch Harbour. The six species of reptile that are native to Britain can all be found on Dorset's heathlands.

Those who watched the popular television series, *The Durrells* will probably associate famous naturalist, Gerald Durrell with the island of Corfu but, in fact, Bournemouth was the place that featured most in his life. He lived in the area both before and after the family's adventures in Greece, and Bournemouth Pier appeared in the first episode of the series as they set off on their travels.

Our journey of exploration begins in Bournemouth and takes a circular route in an anti-clockwise direction, visiting the coastal resorts of Boscombe and Christchurch before heading inland to Wimborne Minster and Kingston Lacy, ending back on the coast at Poole.

Bournemouth Pier (right) was designed by Eugenius Birch and was officially opened by the Lord Mayor of London in 1880. The new iron pier was 838 feet long and cost £21,600; by contrast, the restoration project that began in 1979 cost £1.7 million. Bournemouth is only a hundred miles from London and the railway brought tourists by the trainload to enjoy the sea, sunshine and entertainments on offer. By the early 20th century, the pier offered a bandstand, covered shelters, a popular Punch & Judy show and roller skating, and had been extended to 1000 feet in length. In 1940, a German invasion was feared imminent and the pier was partially demolished as a precaution but was rebuilt and opened again in 1946. The Pier Theatre had been added in the 1960s but closed fifty years later due to declining audiences. It was converted into an indoor adventure centre, which has 25 climbing walls and an aerial obstacle course.

*Above:* Detectorist beneath the pier at dawn.

*p.16:* Wall art by Tech Moon.

Bournemouth is famous for its golden sandy beaches, which stretch for miles and offer views across to the Isle of Wight and Dorset's Isle of Purbeck. The beaches predominantly face south and are sheltered by the cliffs behind, so enjoy a favourable micro-climate. The sea temperatures in the bay are amongst the warmest in Britain. With an average of 1690 hours of sunshine per year, Bournemouth attracts almost seven million visitors.

The West Cliff Lift *(right)* in Bournemouth was built in 1908 and links the seafront with the Bournemouth International Centre. The lift runs on tracks and so is classed as a funicular railway. Each car carries up to twelve people and the ascent offers impressive views of the coast. There are two lifts currently operating in the town, West Cliff and Fisherman's Walk and they run during peak season.

Bournemouth was home to the first municipal beach huts in the UK. Designed and built under the guidance of Frederick Percy Dolamore, they were put up either side of the pier in 1909. A plaque commemorates these purpose-built huts; earlier huts had been converted from old boating sheds or bathing machines. There are now a wide variety of styles stretching along the coast, from traditional wooden huts *(top, middle & right)* to modern pods and lodges.

Bournemouth Land Train operates two routes along the seafront and runs a fleet of five brightly coloured trains *(above)* that start by Bournemouth Pier and take passengers east to Boscombe Pier or west to Alum Chine.

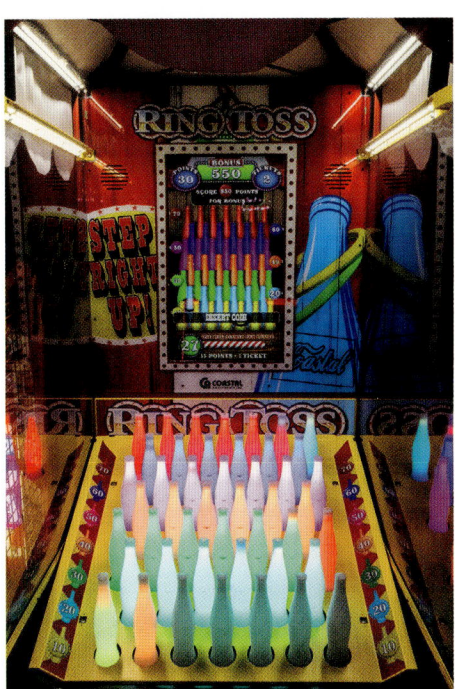

Amusement arcades hold a special place in British culture and there are more than 1200 across the country. The games on offer have changed dramatically over the years with high tech video games offering a very different experience to Whack-a-Mole. Pier Amusements *(left & above)* is a family entertainment centre at the entrance of Bournemouth Pier, which has classic games alongside the most up-to-date.

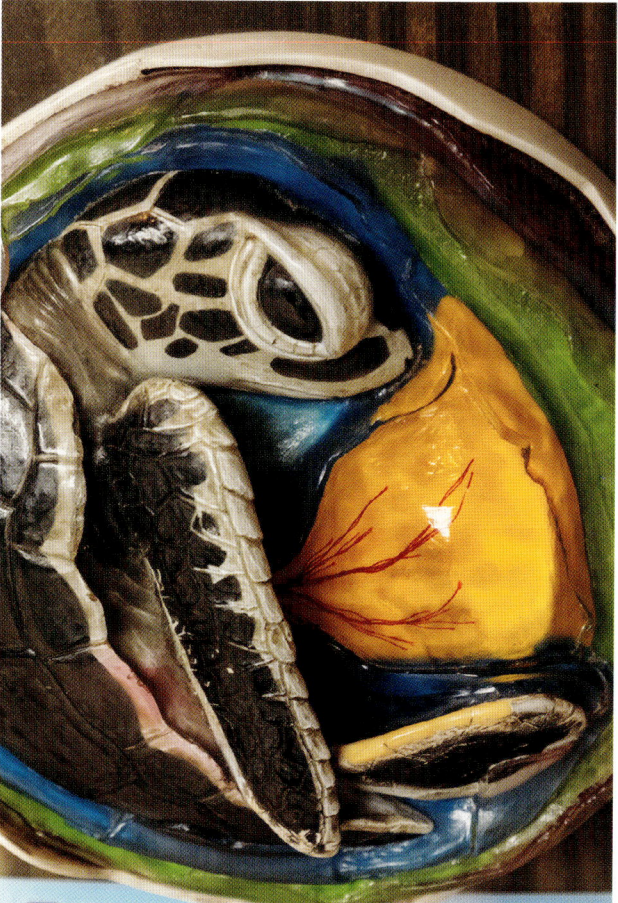

The Oceanarium in Bournemouth is located on the seafront next to the pier and opened in 1998. This aquarium is home to many fascinating creatures and is divided into 11 zones, each with a different theme. Residents include sharks *(above middle)*, stingrays *(top left)*, turtles *(top middle)*, jellyfish *(right)*, iguanas *(above right)* and a colony of Humboldt penguins *(above left)*.

*Top right:* Model showing cross-section of a turtle egg.

Many famous people have enjoyed the sea air at Bournemouth over the years. Author of *The Lord of the Rings*, J R R Tolkien came here on holiday for thirty years before retiring to the area, and The Beatles played here frequently. The Pier Theatre, which opened in 1959, had its heyday in the following decades with summer seasons full of household names including Terry Scott, Thora Hird, Sid James, Danny la Rue and Dick Emery.

*Above & right:* Bournemouth Pier.

*pp.40-41:* View from the pier at dusk.

One of Bournemouth's most interesting buildings is the Russell-Cotes Museum & Art Gallery *(left & above)*, which sits at the top of the East Cliff and enjoys panoramic views of the sea.

Merton Russell-Cotes moved to Bournemouth with his wife Annie in 1876 and became mayor in 1894. He gave East Cliff Hall to Annie as a birthday present in 1901, and they travelled the world collecting beautiful objects to fill it. They later decided to gift their home and its contents to the people of Bournemouth. It was renamed in their honour and is the main museum in the town.

As well as being fascinated by curiosities, Merton and Annie Russell-Cotes had a passion for Victorian art and amassed a notable collection that is on display in the museum. Three purpose-built galleries were added to East Cliff Hall between 1916 and 1919 and these allowed larger works to be displayed. The construction was paid for by Annie and the galleries officially opened on Merton and Annie's 59th wedding anniversary. A fourth gallery was added later. Artists whose work is represented include Dante Gabriel Rossetti, Evelyn de Morgan, Albert Joseph Moore and Sir Edwin Landseer.

*Top right:* Gallery II   *Above right: Repose* (1899) by Géza Vastagh.   *Above left: Love Locked Out* (1890-1910) by Henry Justice Ford.

*Right:* The Main Hall.

p.38 clockwise from top left: *The Butterfly* (1893) by Luis Ricardo Faléro; *Venetian Water Carrier* (1890) by Eugene von Blaas; *Grazzia* (1872) by Rafaello Sorbi; *The Fortune Teller*; *'Beware of a Dark Lady'* (1940) by Frank Cadogan Cowper; *The Chosen Five* (1885) by Edwin Longsden Long.

p.39 clockwise from top left: *The Reception* (late 1880s–early 1900s); *George Bernard Shaw* (1928) by Kathleen Scott; *Napoleon* (19th century)

Eye rejoices in
from Hour to

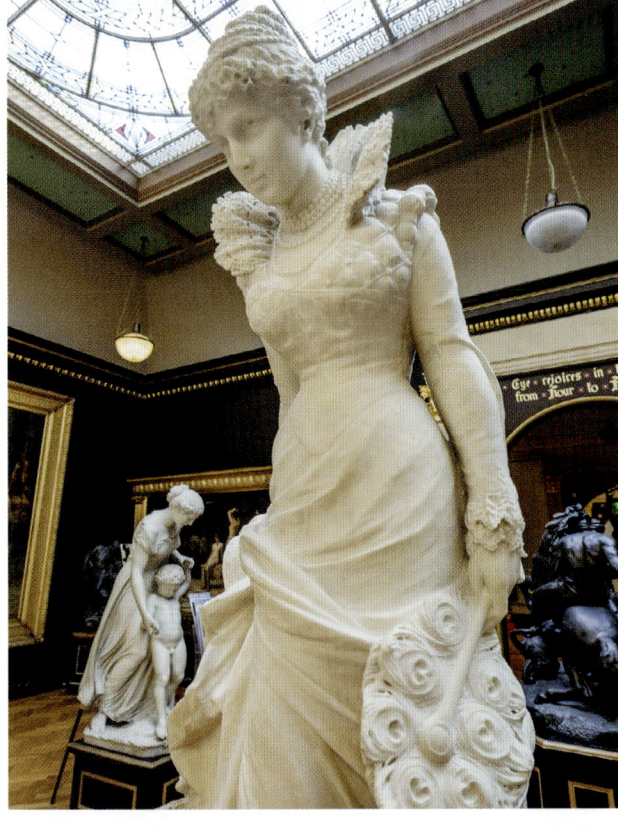

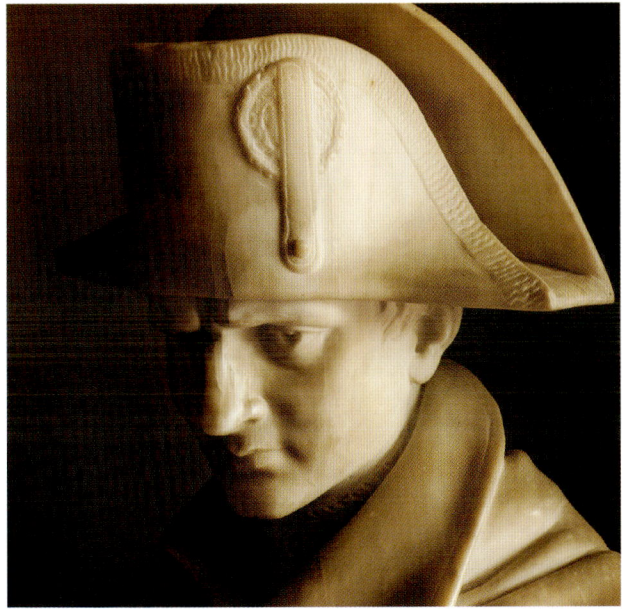

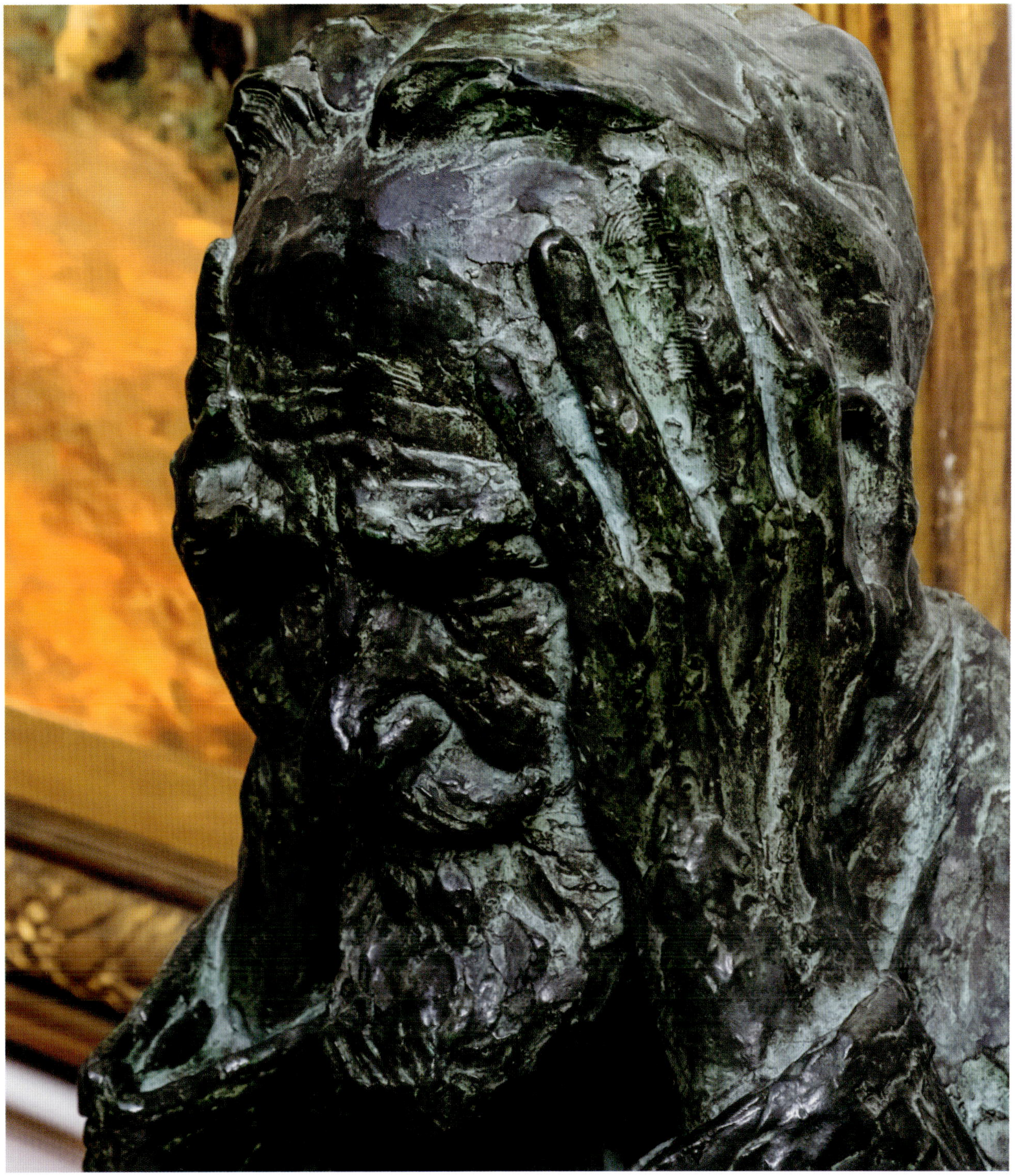

Bournemouth Air Festival takes place over four days at the end of August. It has been held since 2008 and has entertained nearly 10.5 million people over the last 15 years, with dramatic air displays plus a range of activities along the seafront. Aircraft taking part have included the Red Arrows *(far left & left bottom)*, as well as Typhoons and the Battle of Britain Memorial Flight *(left middle)*.

*Left top:* Wingwalkers at the Air Festival.

*Above:* Memorial to Flt Lt Jon Egging, a Red Arrows pilot who was tragically killed at the 2011 Festival.

The seaside resort of Boscombe is a suburb of Bournemouth and adjoins the town on its eastern side. Boscombe Pier *(left)* is separated from its neighbour in Bournemouth by a mile or so, and also has Victorian origins. It was designed by Archibald Smith and was officially opened by the 8th Duke of Argyll in 1889, although the pier head was not added until 1926. It has undergone a number of changes since, partly due to fluctuations in demand. In 2008, the pier and surrounding area were extensively renovated and the derelict building at the end of the pier was demolished and replaced with a viewing platform, which is also used by fishermen.

*Above:* Street art in Boscombe by Tech Moon.

Boscombe is full of local character and has a mixture of architectural styles ranging from the Victorian to Art Deco and the modern. There is a market that opens on Thursdays and Saturdays and sells fresh local produce, and a quirky range of independent shops in The Royal Arcade and surrounding streets.

*Above:* Street art in Boscombe by Tech Moon.

*Right:* Chaplin's with mural by Vivien Hoffman, helped by Kizzi B Creative.

On Dorset's eastern boundary is the town of Christchurch, which sits between Bournemouth and the New Forest in neighbouring Hampshire. It is home to one of the finest parish churches in the country and reputedly the longest, measuring 95 metres from east to west. Christchurch Priory *(left & top)* was built on land between the River Stour and the River Avon and looks over Christchurch Harbour. It dates from the 11th century but took many centuries to complete and it wasn't until the first half of the 16th century that it had the form seen today.

*Above left:* The Nave.

*Above right:* Stained glass (late 1990s) by Paul Quail in Cloister Way.

Christchurch began as an early Saxon settlement. Originally called Twyneham, it was renamed following the construction of the priory in the 11th century. It now has a population of thirty-one thousand and is a popular tourist destination.

*Right:* Christchurch Priory and the River Stour.

*Top:* The River Stour.

*Middle:* Church Street and Christchurch Priory.

*Above:* Castle Street and Christchurch Castle at night.

Permission to hold a weekly market was first granted to Christchurch in the 12th century and this is now held in the High Street every Monday. Around fifty stalls offer a wide variety of food, household items, toys and collectibles *(left & above)*.

A food festival has been held in the town at the end of May for more than twenty years. Based around Christchurch Quay, the three-day event includes an international food market and demonstrations by celebrity chefs.

Christchurch Castle is a Norman motte and bailey castle that was built in the 12th century. Only the ruins of the keep and a chamber block, known as the Norman House, remain standing. The castle passed to the Crown in 1293 and later came under attack during the English Civil War. It was lost to the Parliamentarians and subsequently demolished in 1651.
The ditch has now been filled in and there is a bowling green and gardens within the bailey.

The Norman House *(above)* was built within the bailey of Christchurch Castle around 1160 and is a rare survivor of a domestic dwelling from this period. It would have provided impressive accommodation for the 2nd Earl of Devon and his family when it was built but became home to the constable responsible for the site's security after the castle passed to the Crown. The chimney *(right)* is of particular importance and is one of very few Norman examples still in existence.

The harbour at Christchurch is sheltered from the English Channel by the natural headland of Hengistbury Head and a sand spit called Mudeford Sandbank *(left)*. More than 340 beach huts form two rows along the length of the spit. These are privately owned and very desirable, despite the fact that overnight stays are only permitted in peak season. Demand far outstrips supply and prices can reach well over £450,000, a big increase on the average of £80,000 just twenty years ago.

*Above:* Fisherman repairing crab and lobster pots at Mudeford Quay.

*pp.54-55:* Path on Hengistbury Head, looking west to Christchurch and Bournemouth.

Highcliffe Castle *(left & above right)* was built in the 1830s and is an important survivor of Gothic Revival architecture. Now Grade I listed, it was built by Lord Stuart de Rothesay in a clifftop location and medieval stonework and stained glass salvaged from abbeys in Normandy were used in its construction. The castle stayed with descendants of the family until passing to a very distant cousin, Edward Worley in 1891. During Worley's ownership, the American-born retail magnate, Harry Gordon Selfridge rented the castle for six years from 1916. From the 1950s, it suffered decline and eventually passed into the ownership of Christchurch Council in 1977. With help from English Heritage, the castle underwent a long-running programme of conservation and repair. It now hosts events, including weddings, and opens to visitors throughout the year.

*Above right:* The Jesse Window in the Great Hall.

Leaving the coast and heading north-west, away from the county border, leads to Wimborne Minster, a market town with a parish church *(right & above)* of the same name. The oldest parts of the church are from the Saxon period, but the design is mainly Norman with later extensions and alterations. It has two towers, one at the centre and one at the west end, which was added in the 15th century. There used to be a spire on the original tower, but this fell in a storm around 1600 and was not replaced.

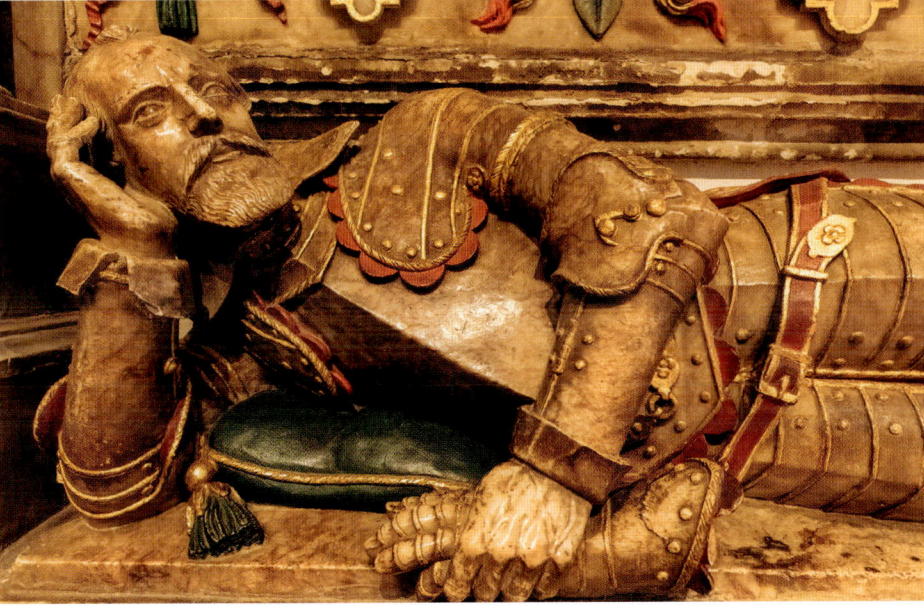

The interior of Wimborne Minster has many historic features, including a chained library, which was founded in 1686. It is one of the first public libraries in England and the collection includes early books on subjects such as gardening, law, medicine and construction, as well as theology.

*Left:* Ceiling of the Central Tower.

*p.63* clockwise from top left: The Nave; the Town Mayor's Serjant and Crier, Chris Brown; the Pulpit (1886); Flower Festival display; Tomb of Edmund Uvedale.

Just outside Wimborne Minster is the country house and estate of Kingston Lacy *(left)*. Built in the 1660s, it was owned by the Bankes family and stayed with their descendants until bequeathed to the National Trust in 1982. The building was designed by the architect, Sir Roger Pratt and was remodelled by Sir Charles Barry in the 19th century; it is now Grade I listed. The grounds are also considered of historic interest and feature a fernery and kitchen garden, as well as a formal parterre, all surrounded by acres of parkland and woodland.

*Above:* The Drawing Room.

The interior of Kingston Lacy has been shaped by generations of the Bankes family, but it was William John Bankes who oversaw the most significant changes when he inherited the estate in 1834. He had the exterior of the building clad with local stone, which changed its appearance dramatically from the original red brick. William John was inspired by Venetian palaces and wanted to create an aesthetic masterpiece at Kingston Lacy, with art and objects collected from around the world. He travelled around Europe and the Near East and developed a passion for Egyptian antiquities. Kingston Lacy now houses one of the National Trust's most important collections of art, with works by masters including Titian and Rubens.

*p.66 left to right:* the Library; the Spanish Room; the Saloon. *p.67 left to right:* the Saloon; Statue of Charles I; the State Bedroom.

The final stop on this anti-clockwise circuit is Poole, a coastal town that adjoins the western edge of Bournemouth. A popular tourist resort, Poole *(left)* benefits from a sheltered, natural harbour and an interesting history. During World War II, Poole was an important embarkation point for the D-Day landings and a plaque commemorates the more than 300 craft that left the quays and set sail for Normandy as part of Operation Overlord *(above)*.

In 1907, Robert Baden-Powell set up an experimental camp for boys on Brownsea Island in Poole Harbour. He wanted to test out ideas for his book, *Scouting for Boys*. This camp became the start of the Scout Movement, and a statue of Baden-Powell stands on Poole Quay *(top)*.

The town of Poole has long been famous for the pottery that was first produced here in 1873, when Jesse Carter bought the East Quay Works. Changes of name and premises followed but the high standard of craftmanship continued. It wasn't until 1963 that the company became officially known as Poole Pottery Ltd. The vibrant Delphis designs were developed and became instantly fashionable in the Swinging '60s. The pottery celebrated their centenary in 1973 and were one of Poole's biggest employers at this time. However, they closed suddenly in 2006 and production was transferred to Stoke-on-Trent. The important link with the town of Poole was retained and a studio shop opened on the quay where the first pottery stood.

*pp.70-71: Studio Poole on Poole Quays.*

At the entrance to Poole Harbour is Sandbanks *(p.74-75)*, one of the most exclusive addresses in England. This is Poole's most affluent neighbourhood, where the average house price exceeds £1.5 million and a price tag of £8 million is not unique. Famous residents include former football manager, Harry Redknapp and presenter/comedian, Karl Pilkington. The beach has been a Blue Flag award winner for over thirty years and offers soft, golden sand and expansive views across the harbour to Poole and along the coast. Sandbanks can be reached by road from the east or via the Sandbanks Ferry *(p.75 bottom right)*, which links to Studland on the Isle of Purbeck.

*pp.72-73:* Aerial view of Sandbanks.

# THE PRETTY PENINSULA

Moving away from the south-east conurbation, Dorset has a very different feel. The towns are smaller and there is more countryside to explore. It is one of only ten counties in England without a city and one of a handful with no motorway.

Possibly the biggest jewel in Dorset's weighty crown is the Jurassic Coast, which runs for 95 miles from Studland Bay along the south coast into Devon. This coastline was deemed so significant that it was made a UNESCO World Heritage Site in 2001 and is still England's only natural landscape to be included on this globally-recognised list.

Geology underpins the importance of the region, both literally and metaphorically. The rock layers date from the beginning of the Triassic period, through the Jurassic to the Cretaceous; a time span of more than 185 million years. It is the only place that rocks from these three periods can be seen in one area and millions of visitors travel from around the world to explore this fascinating piece of Earth's history.

The Jurassic Coast walk is a section of the South-West Coast path, which is the longest National Trail in England. Studland Bay is a start point for both and this is located on the eastern side of Dorset's Isle of Purbeck.

The name 'Isle of Purbeck' is something of a misnomer, as it is not an island but a peninsula, bordered by the English Channel to the south and east and Poole Harbour to the north. Its entire Channel-facing coastline is part of the Jurassic Coast and includes the famous chalk stacks known as Old Harry Rocks. But the Isle of Purbeck is not just famous for its coastline. It is also home to the pretty town of Swanage and has popular heritage attractions that include the dramatic ruins of Corfe Castle and the steam trains of the Swanage Railway.

Although Swanage is the only town officially in Purbeck, Wareham is just on the northern border and has strong connections with its neighbouring villages on the Isle, so is often considered as part of the family.

The flora is also of note, with stunning display of wildflowers thriving on the different geological habitats. The county flower of Dorset is the Dorset heath, a species of heather that flowers in mid-summer. It thrives on damp heathland, such as that found on Hartland Moor near Wareham. The Early Spider Orchid, a protected plant that is classed as nationally scarce, also grows abundantly on the Isle of Purbeck.

The area has long been famous for the quarrying of Purbeck Marble. This fossiliferous limestone has been dug from the earth for centuries and appears in buildings around the country, including Beverley Minster, London's Temple Church and Ely Cathedral. It is not a true marble, but can be finely polished, creating a marble-like finish. The thin seam of rock runs all the way across the Isle of Purbeck from Worbarrow Tout near Tyneham to Peveril Point above Swanage.

The pretty town of Wareham sits between the River Frome and the River Piddle, eight miles south-west of Poole. It is one of very few Saxon-walled settlements remaining in England today. The ancient earth ramparts that surround the town are thought to have been built by Alfred the Great in the 9th century to protect Wareham, which was strategically important, from invading Danes. The town is now popular as a gateway to the Jurassic Coast and its riverside location *(left)* attracts tourists wishing to enjoy a boat trip out to Poole Harbour. A market is held on Wareham Quay *(above)* every Saturday, offering a range of local produce and collectibles. Thomas Hardy used Wareham as the basis of the town Anglebury in his novels.

Just behind the Old Granary on Wareham Quay stands the Priory Church of Lady St Mary (p.78). This parish church (right) has Anglo-Saxon origins and is possibly the burial place of King Beorthric who was King of Wessex and died in 802 AD. The church organ (top right) dates from 1883 and was gifted by the widow of Miles Rodgett JP, in his memory. The impressive east window was installed by Clayton and Bell between 1886 and 1890 (top left).

One of the oldest buildings in Wareham is the church of St Martin on the Walls (bottom left). This Anglo-Saxon church is Grade I listed and sits on the north walls of the town. The present building dates from circa 1030 and is the most complete example from this period in Dorset. Inside the church is a near life-sized effigy of T E Lawrence, more famously known as Lawrence of Arabia, which was installed in the 20th century (bottom right). It was carved by his friend and war artist, Eric Kennington and was originally intended for St Paul's Cathedral. The church is still used for worship, with services held once a week.

One of Dorset's most famous landmarks is the romantic ruin of Corfe Castle, which stands on a hill above a village of the same name. The castle was built soon after the Norman invasion of 1066 and would have reinforced William the Conqueror's power over the defeated local population. The castle passed into private ownership in the 16th century and was owned by the Bankes family during the English Civil War. They were supporters of the King and fought doggedly to defend themselves against the Parliamentarians but eventually lost the fight. An Act of Parliament was passed, and the castle was demolished. The ruined castle was later returned to the family and remained in their hands until 1982 when it was given to the National Trust.

The ruined castle provides a stunning backdrop to the village *(top right)* and is also an excellent viewpoint from which to see the layout of the settlement *(above and top left)* and the surrounding countryside *(right)*. The village is sometimes incorrectly referred to as 'Corfe' but is properly called 'Corfe Castle', which can be confusing for visitors. Found halfway between Wareham and Swanage, the village is a popular tourist destination. The buildings are primarily built of local Purbeck limestone and a cross commemorating the Diamond Jubilee of Queen Victoria sits in the Square, which links the two main streets at their north end. The castle is visited by up to quarter of a million people a year and is thought to be the model for Kirrin Castle in the *Famous Five* books by Enid Blyton.

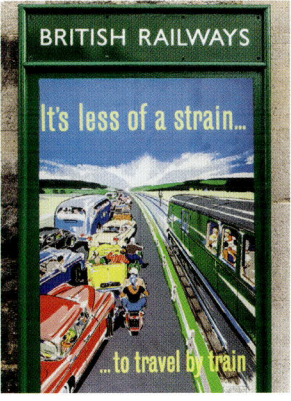
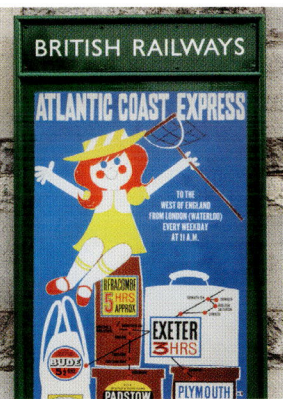

The Swanage Railway is a heritage line that operates a timetable of steam and diesel services along the 5.5 miles of track between Norden and Swanage. One of the intermediate stops is at Corfe Castle *(pp.86-87)* and the sight of a train steaming past the castle ruins is a magnet for photographers. The branch line between Wareham and Swanage originally opened in 1885 but closed to passengers in 1972, with the last train running on the 1st of January in that year. Freight trains did continue to run for some time, but part of the line had been lifted. It took many years of hard work by dedicated volunteers to restore a section of original line and relink it to the national rail network. The railway now contributes more that £15 million per year to the local economy.

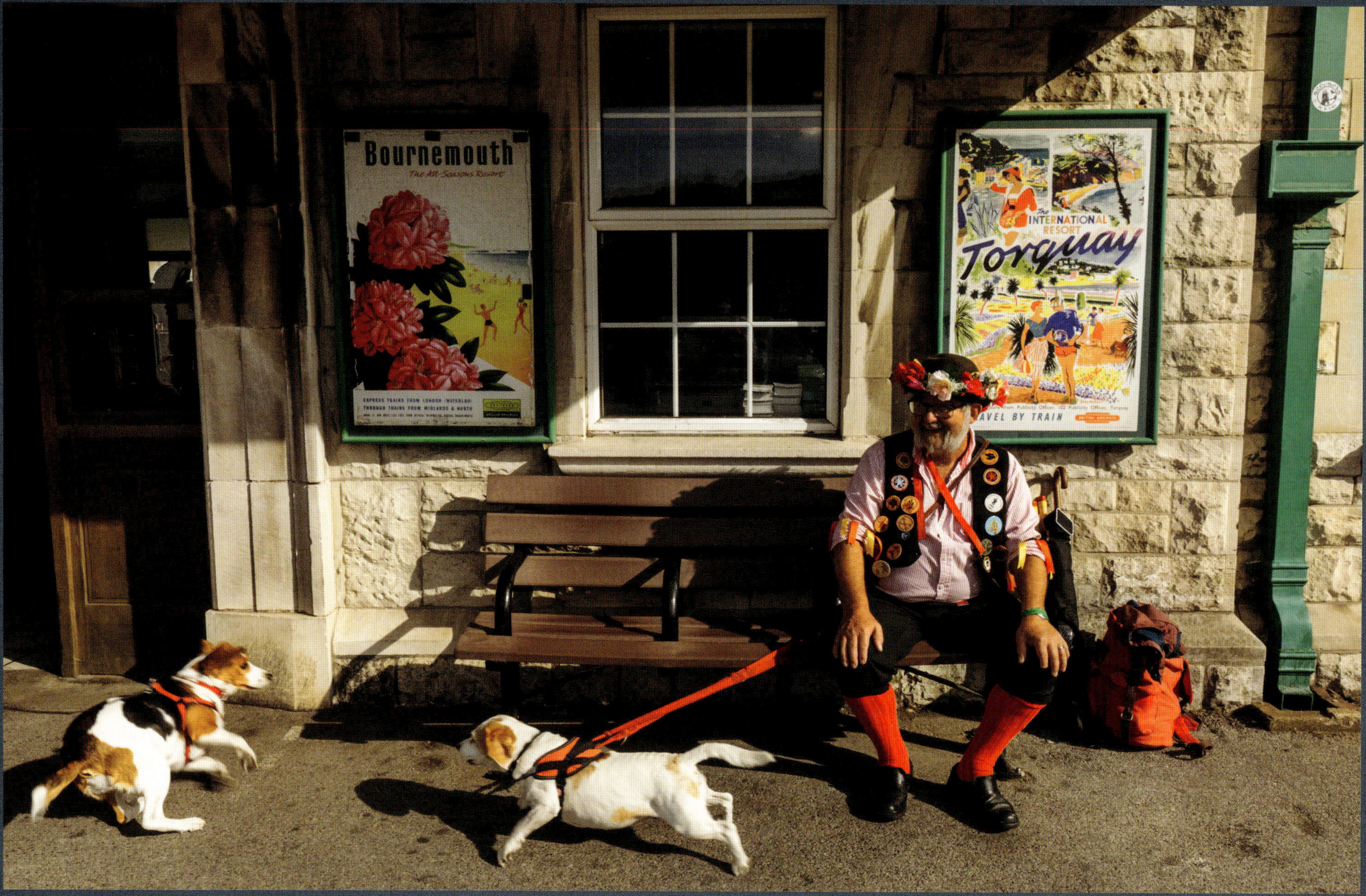
Bournemouth
The All-Seasons Resort
The International Resort
Torquay

STATION SHOP
BRITISH RAILWAYS
TORQUAY
IN GLORIOUS DEVON
TRAVEL BY RAIL
FOR LONDON FOOTBALL
SOUTHERN ELECTRIC
FREQUENT ELECTRIC TRAINS
EASE THE STRAIN — GO BY TRAIN

7P 5FA
34028

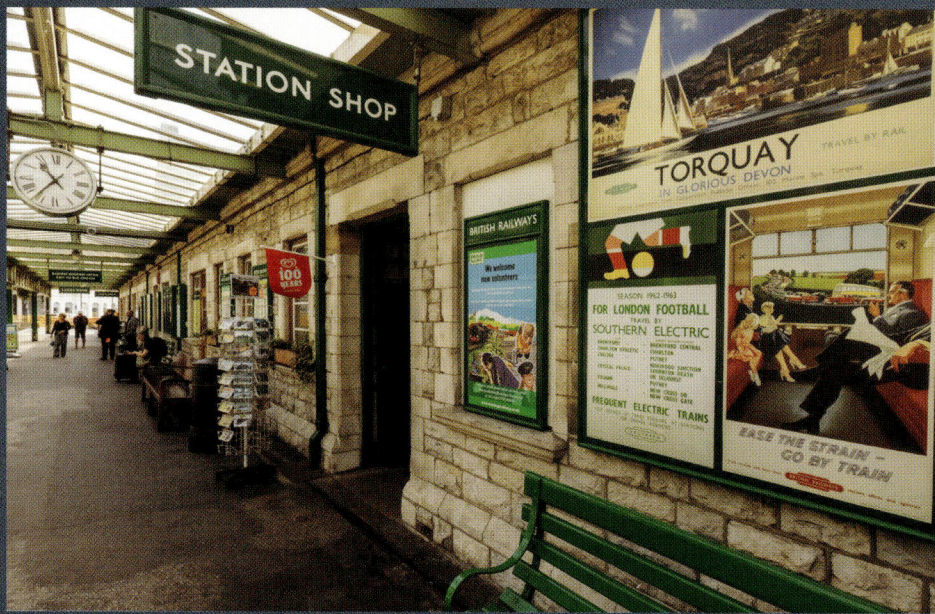

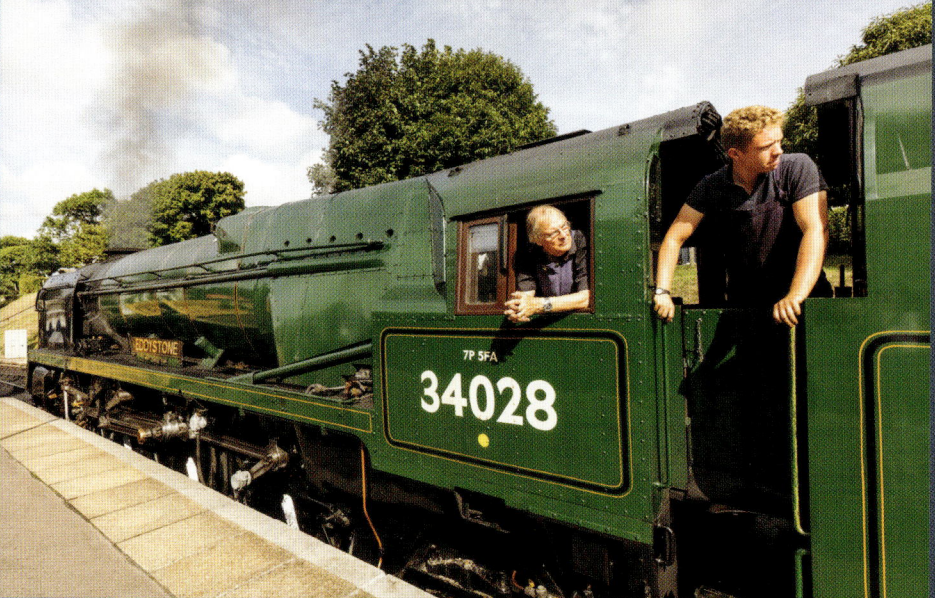

The seaside terminus of the Swanage Railway is Swanage station, which is in the centre of town and within strolling distance of the beach. Redolent of times gone by, with traditional paintwork and colourful posters *(left & bottom left)*, the station evokes a nostalgia for summer holidays of the past.

Swanage Railway has eight steam locomotives, although not all are in service. It also has special visitors, including the *Flying Scotsman* on its recent centenary tour.

*Bottom right & right:* SR 4-6-2 'West Country' Class No. 34028 *Eddystone*.

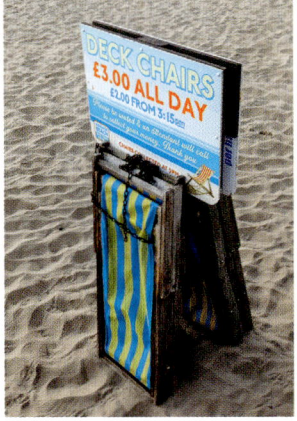

Swanage is known for its beaches, with vast stretches of golden sand and shallow water that are perfect for holidaymakers. After the arrival of the railway in the 1880s, the town became a popular resort, and an increasing number of wealthy travellers made the journey down from London. Tourism remains the town's primary industry today and the resident population figure of under ten thousand nearly doubles as the visitors arrive. The seafront is home to a number of colourful beach huts. There are sixty huts on Shore Road in the centre of Swanage and these belong to the Town Council and are available for hire.

Swanage is the only town on the Isle of Purbeck, as Wareham is just outside the northern boundary. It is on the eastern side of the island and faces east, looking out over Swanage Bay to the English Channel. The beach has been awarded Blue Flag status and the promenade is partly pedestrianised in the summer. It is an ideal base for walkers, with Ballard Down and Old Harry Rocks to the north and Durlston Country Park and Nature Reserve to the south.

*Left & above:* Views over Swanage Bay at dawn.

There is a small Museum & Heritage Centre in the centre of Swanage that has displays and exhibits explaining the history of the town. The museum occupies a prime site in The Square and is built on what used to be an old stone yard known as the 'bankers'. Outside is a mosaic floor roundel *(right)* made in pebbles by Maggy Howarth. The stone industry was very important in the development of Swanage before the town became a resort.

*Above right:* One-man band.  *Above left:* Santa-Fe Fun Park on Shore Road.

Every year, Swanage hosts a Folk Festival that attracts visitors from far and wide. For three days in September the town is full of dancing and music – and a lot of interesting characters. The festival has been running for more than thirty years and centres around Sandpit Field on Shore Road. It's always held on the second weekend after the August Bank Holiday and the main days are the Saturday and Sunday. This is when the Morris dancers display their skills, with bells jingling and sticks banging.

Sides of Morris dancers come from all over England to enjoy the seaside fun at Swanage, but the festival also showcases traditional folk dances from Bulgaria, Slovakia, Czechia, the Middle East and Ireland, with more than sixty groups taking part. Headline bands appear in the marquee at Sandpit Field and there are evening concerts over the weekend.

The Durlston Country Park and National Nature Reserve is just a mile or so from Swanage and its clifftop location offers far-reaching views. Extending over 320 acres, the area is popular with walkers and has a number of points of interest. These include Anvil Point lighthouse, Tilly Whim Caves and Durlston Castle, which was originally built as a restaurant for visitors to the estate by George Burt in the 1880s *(above left & right)*. Burt also commissioned the Great Globe in the same decade *(left)*. This sphere of limestone weighs 40 tons and has a diameter of three metres. Made of Portland stone, it is one of the largest stone spheres in the world. Its surface is engraved with a world map and readers of Rachel McLean's Dorset Crime series may recognise it as the scene of a gruesome murder - fortunately only fictional. Durlston Country Park is an important wildlife habitat attracting over thirty-three species of butterfly and playing host to more than 250 different types of bird during the year.

The distinctive outlines of the Old Harry Rocks *(left, top & p.76)* mark the most easterly point of Dorset's Jurassic Coast. These chalk formations are found at Handfast Point below Ballard Down, at the southern end of Studland Bay. Many thousands of years ago, they were part of a range of chalk hills that stretched to the Isle of Wight, but sea erosion eventually formed the shapes seen today. These will continue to change over time, as old columns (called stacks) collapse and new ones are formed. Old Harry used to have a neighbouring stack, known as his wife, but this fell in 1896, leaving only a stump. There are more sea stacks nearby, off the cliffs of Ballard Down *(above)*.

In the village of Kimmeridge on the south side of the Isle of Purbeck is The Etches Collection Museum of Jurassic Marine Life *(left, top & above left)*. This important collection stems from the passion of one man, Steve Etches, whose fascination with fossils began at the age of five. He now has more than 2800 examples, all from the Kimmeridge Bay area, and that number continues to grow. The most scientifically important and visually exciting of these are on display in a striking, purpose-built museum, which opened in 2016 and cost an estimated £5 million.

*Above right & middle right:* Dorset landscape paintings by Caz Scott, who has had an artist residency at The Etches Collection.

About a mile from The Etches Collection and the source of many of its exhibits is Kimmeridge Bay, an area whose geology is of global importance. This sheltered, rocky bay has a large, wave-cut platform below the cliffs and rock pools form that are perfect hunting grounds for enthusiasts of marine life and ecology. Fossils can be found in the flat clay-beds known as the Kimmeridge Ledges, which are just to the south-east of the bay.

On the cliff top overlooking Kimmeridge Bay stands Clavell Tower, built as a folly and observatory by the Reverend John Richards Clavell around 1830. It was later used as a lookout by the local coastguard but was then left empty and became increasingly derelict. Now owned by The Landmark Trust, the tower faced a further threat to its survival in the early 2000s. The sea was gradually eroding the cliff below and the building was in real danger of falling into the sea. A rescue mission began in 2006 and the tower was completely dismantled and then reassembled a little further inland. Work was completed early in 2008 and Clavell Tower is now a holiday let with spectacular views of the Jurassic Coast.

To the east of Kimmeridge and south of the village of Wool is Lulworth Castle *(left)*, which dates from the early 17th century. It was originally built as a hunting lodge in the style of a fortified castle, designed to impress the wealthy visitors who were entertained here. The castle was acquired by the Weld family in the 1640s and became their family seat for the following centuries. A disastrous fire in 1929 put the future of the building at risk, but the Weld Family and English Heritage worked together to make the building safe and to discover more about its history. Now a tourist attraction, Lulworth Castle opened to the public in 1998.

*Above, Interior views.*

A return to the Jurassic Coast leads to Lulworth Cove *(above, left & right)*, considered one of the most interesting places in the world for geologists but also a honeypot for tourists, with over half a million visitors a year. The cove formed because of a weakness in the Portland stone formation at its mouth. This fault would have been exploited by the constant action of the sea, eventually allowing the water access to the softer rocks beyond that were more easily eroded, resulting in the circular cove seen today. The rocks at the front of the cove are around 150 million years old, but those at the back are more than 50 million years younger.

The road leading to the Lulworth Cove is lined with businesses catering for the many tourists visiting the area. The Lulworth Cove Inn *(left)* is perfectly located to provide refreshment for the hot and weary. Opposite are eight Coastguard Cottages that were built in 1824. Although smuggling was on the decline by this time, there is record of a Chief Officer of the Coastguard who was attacked by a gang of smugglers near Lulworth in 1832 and then thrown over the cliff.

Bovington Camp, just to the north of Wool, is a military base for the British Army. Together with Lulworth Camp, it was established in 1899 for infantry, before becoming a training area for the newly renamed Tank Corps towards the end of the First World War. Inextricably linked to the Royal Armoured Corps, Bovington was the RAC Centre from 1947 until 1999. It is now called the Armour Centre as it provides training in tracked armoured vehicles across the whole army, and not just for the RAC, although it is still their home.

Following the end of the war in 1918, the future of the Tank Corps was in doubt. The personnel in Bovington and nearby camps fell from 16,000 to just over 2,000 and tanks were sent across the country as war trophies for display. However, some were kept, possibly at the suggestion of Rudyard Kipling, and these later became the start of The Tank Museum *(above & right)*, which opened to the public in 1947.

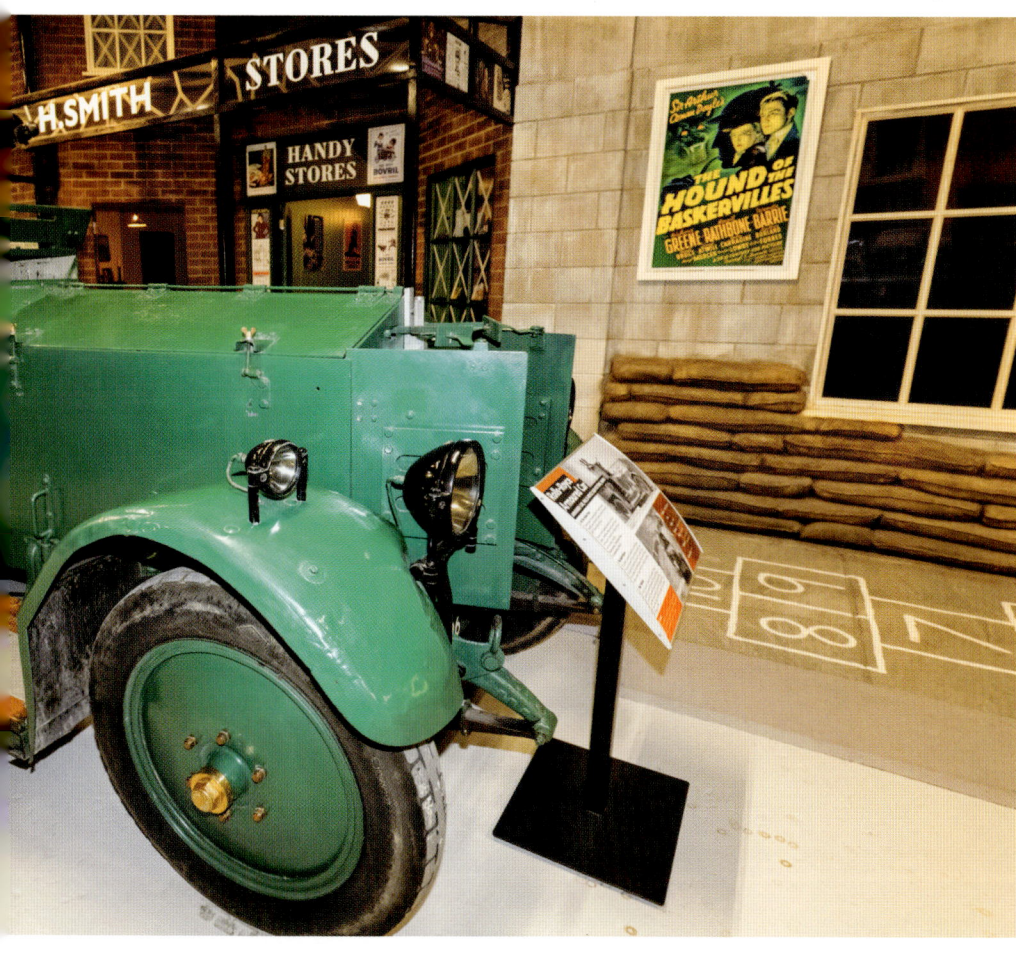

The Tank Museum at Bovington is home to the world's finest collection of tanks and illustrates the history of the armoured fighting vehicle, with numerous exhibitions displayed across seven exhibition halls. The museum now has around 300 tanks from all around the world, some of which are unique survivors of their type. A programme of events also runs throughout the year, including TANKFEST, which sees vehicles from the museum's collection running alongside guest tanks from the British Army.

*Above (top to bottom):* Protection suits for biological warfare; Carrier Pigeon; Last surviving *Mark 1* tank from the Great War.

Monkey World, near Bovington, is not a zoo but a rescue centre for primates. It has worked with governments around the world since 1987 to try to prevent the illegal trade of these animals and it rehabilitates those who have suffered so that they can enjoy a better life within a natural living group. There are over 260 rescued and endangered monkeys, apes and prosimians living on the 65-acre site, many of whom have made appearances on the popular TV shows, *Monkey Business* and the follow-up *Monkey Life*, which are based on the day-to-day work of the centre.

Possibly the most recognisable landmark on the Jurassic Coast is Durdle Door *(above left & right)*, a magnificent limestone arch formed by the power of the waves. The name 'Durdle' is thought to derive from an old English word meaning bore or drill. The coastline is constantly eroding and so the arch will eventually collapse, leaving a sea stack separated from the land – but hopefully not for many years. Unsurprisingly, the beauty of the location makes it a popular choice for film & television makers, with appearances in *Nanny McPhee*, *Wilde* and *Doctor Who*. Although open to the public, it is actually privately owned and is part of the Lulworth Estate.

*Top:* View west to Bat's Head.

*Above right:* Cliff path above Durdle Door, looking to Bat's Head.

*pp.120-121:* Looking east to Man O'War Beach.

# THE TAIL OF WESSEX

One literary name that is inextricably linked with the county of Dorset is that of the writer, Thomas Hardy. Most of his work is set in a fictional region that he called Wessex, with South Wessex sitting at its very heart. This area closely identifies with Dorset, and it was here that Hardy lived and worked for most of his life. He was inspired by the local towns and surrounding scenery and included many of these in his works but changed their names to ones that he created.

Dorchester is the county town of Dorset and was at the centre of much of Hardy's life. He was born in the nearby village of Higher Bockhampton and shared a cottage with his family there until he was a young man. After a short interlude in London, he came back to Dorset, settling in Weymouth before returning to Dorchester in 1881. Hardy finally moved to Max Gate on the outskirts of town four years later and remained there for forty-three years, until his death.

Thomas Hardy's work captured the essence of Dorset in the second half of the 19th century with his descriptive and lyrical writing. Casterbridge, which was based on Dorchester and appeared in one of his most famous novels, The Mayor of Casterbridge, merited the following:

*To birds of the more soaring kind Casterbridge must have appeared on this fine evening as a mosaic-work of subdued reds, browns, greys, and crystals, held together by a rectangular frame of deep green.*

South of Dorchester is the coastal town of Weymouth and the Isle of Portland, which are both part of the Jurassic Coast World Heritage site.

Hardy described Portland as *the peninsular carved by Time out of a single stone;* words that contrast to his softer descriptions of the rest of the county but capture the sense of place in a few well-considered words.

Despite the famous lighthouse that sits at the southern end of the Isle of Portland *(left)*, the challenging waters have been the cause of many wrecks over the centuries, particularly in the days of sail.

Portland Museum has a map which tells of more than 2,000 wrecks of both planes and ships along the Dorset coast, with over 400 documented sites around Portland. The number of wrecks on the west side of the island at the eastern end of Chesil Beach was so high that the name, Deadman's Bay given to the area by Thomas Hardy in his novel *The Well-Beloved*, seemed particularly appropriate.

The development of rocket-fired lines in the 19th century allowed rescue attempts to be tried from shore and this led to a reduction in fatalities, but major wrecks continued well into the 20th century. On a foggy winter's night, despite modern navigation systems, today's sailors are still glad to see the flashing light of the Portland Bill lighthouse guiding them safely on their way.

Eight miles to the east of Dorset's county town, Dorchester is the small village of Tolpuddle *(left)*. Its population may be less than five hundred, but the village holds an important place in the history of the fight for workers' rights. In 1834, farm labourers in the local area formed a trade union to try to improve standards. Their pay had been cut several times and they only received six shillings for a week's hard toil, equivalent to about fifty pounds today. Six of the leaders were arrested and charged with taking an illegal oath. The sentence was transportation to Australia for seven years. The men became known as the Tolpuddle Martyrs. Demonstrations were held in London to protest against their sentence and a petition was raised, eventually leading to free pardons for the men and a free passage home. This helped to establish the right of workers to organise trade unions. A memorial to the Martyrs *(below)*, created by Thompson Dagnall, sits outside the Tolpuddle Martyrs Museum in the village *(bottom)*.

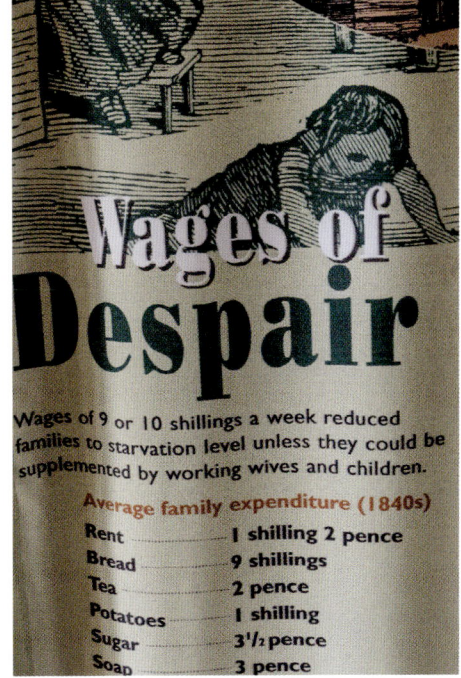

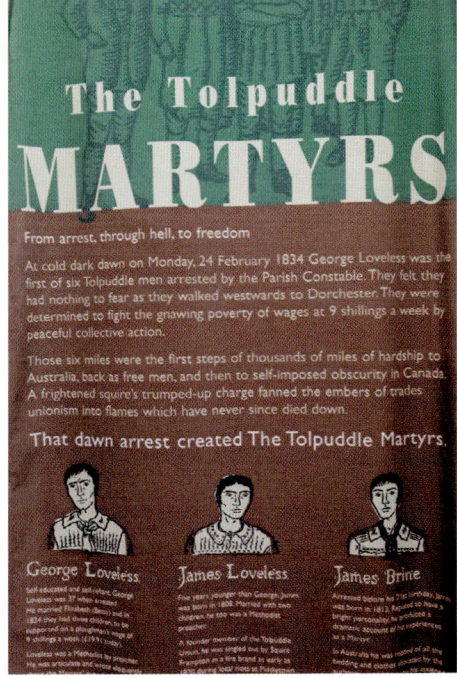

Open to visitors throughout the year, the manor house of Athelhampton is amongst the finest examples of Tudor architecture in England. The manor was recorded in the Domesday Book but the house dates from the 15th century and is Grade I listed, with a magnificent Great Hall that has an intricate hammerbeam roof. Athelhampton has had many owners over the centuries and was bought, in 1890, by Alfred Cart De Lafontaine. He commissioned Francis Inigo Thomas to create the architectural gardens that still survive today. Thomas Hardy lived in nearby Higher Bockhampton and was frequently entertained by Lafontaine. Inspired by Athelhampton, Hardy immortalised it in a short story and a poem. The house also featured in the 1972 film *Sleuth*, as well as Julian Fellowes' film, *From Time to Time*.

Hardy's Cottage *(right)* nestles in the centre of a traditional garden at the end of Cuckoo Lane in Higher Bockhampton. Built by Thomas Hardy's great-grandfather, it was home to the famous author who was born here in 1840. Hardy lived here all his early life, leaving to study architecture in London when he was twenty-two, although he returned a few years later. His earlier novels, including *Far from the Madding Crowd*, were written in the cottage, which is now cared for by the National Trust. Visitors can wander through the rooms *(above)* to see where Hardy worked, and then explore the surrounding woodland that provided inspiration for his writing.

Dorchester has been the county town of Dorset for more than 700 years and grew up on the south side of the River Frome. Although inland, it is only five miles from the coast. With a current population of around 20,000, it has a long history dating back to Roman times. The town suffered from a number of fires in the 1600s and 1700s that destroyed earlier buildings and resulted in the Georgian architecture that still prevails today. The infamous trial of the Tolpuddle Martyrs took place in what is now the Shire House Historic Courtyard Museum *(bottom left)*, and visitors can ascend the stairs from the cells to the dock but, unlike the Martyrs, they are then free to leave. Shire Hall was Dorset's county hall and courthouse for over 150 years from the late 18th century and writer, Thomas Hardy was once a magistrate here.

*Left:* Dorset Museum, St Peter's Church, Corn Exchange.  *Top left:* Bandstand in Borough Gardens.  *Top right:* The King's Arms Hotel.  *Bottom right:* High East Street.

Dorchester's Borough Gardens first opened to the public in the summer of 1896. Based on designs by William Goldring of Kew, they were completely restored around fifteen years ago and officially re-opened by the creator of Downton Abbey, Julian Fellowes in 2007. The Victorian bandstand and clock tower *(left)*, which date from 1898, are particular highlights of the park. Near to the gardens and by the Top O'Town Roundabout stands another reminder of Dorset's most famous son, Thomas Hardy *(above)*. Hardy was both a novelist and a poet and his works *(below)* are regularly adapted for film and television.

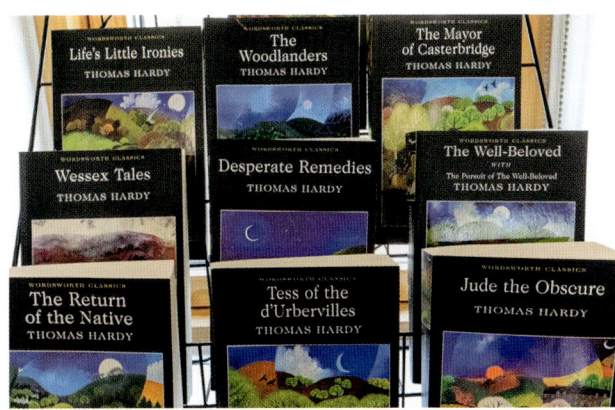

The story of Thomas Hardy *(top left)* continues at the Dorset County Museum in Dorchester's High West Street. Just over ten years after he got married to Emma Gifford *(above right)*, Hardy designed a house which his brother then built for the couple on the outskirts of Dorchester. It was called Max Gate and the Hardys moved there in 1885. A reconstruction of his study has been created in the museum *(above left)*. Hardy and his wife Emma later became estranged, and contemporaries noted that they did not get on well together. Emma died in 1912 and Hardy remarried two years later. He passed away at Max Gate in 1928 and the house is now in the care of the National Trust.

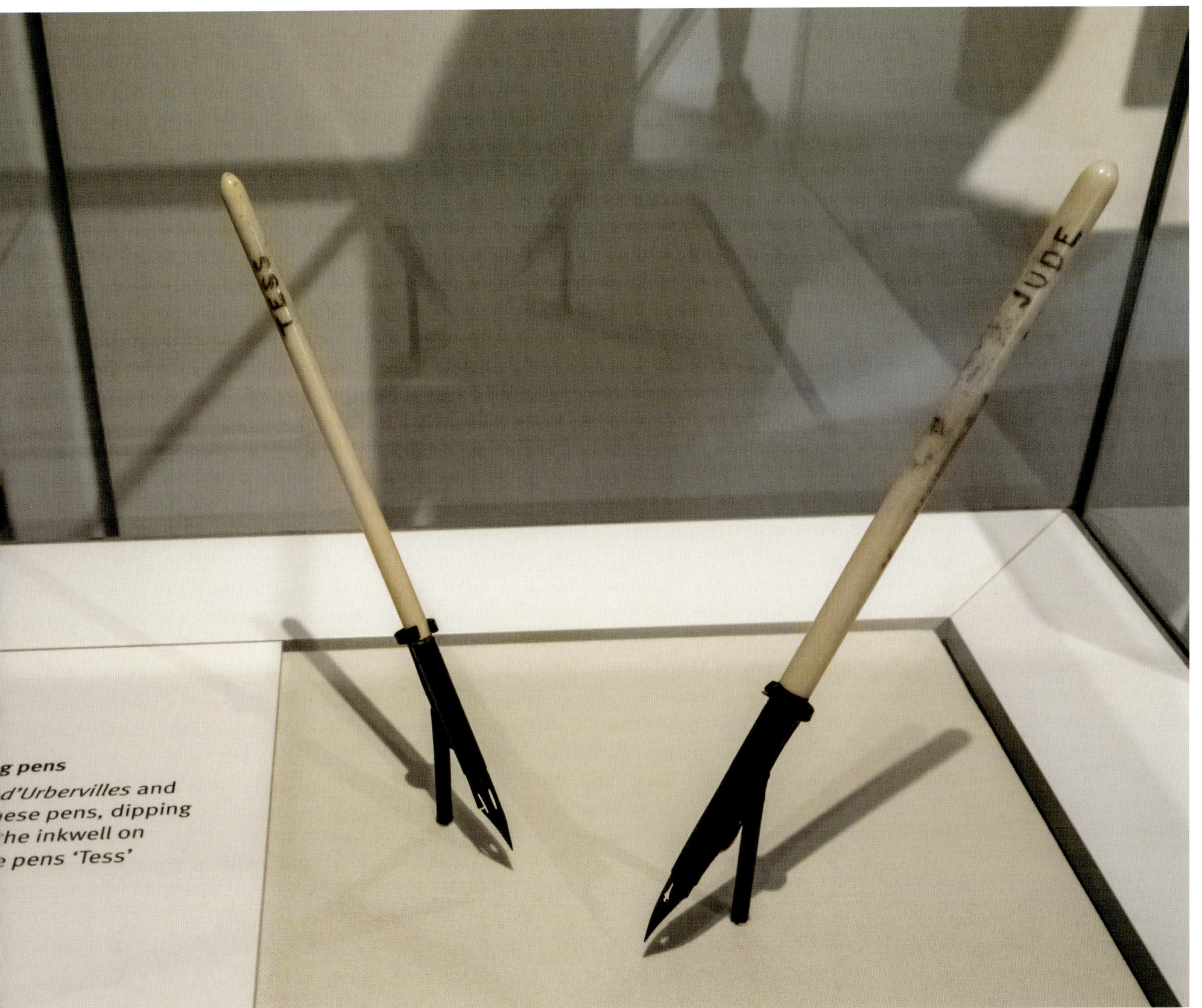

Displays in the museum include the pens that Hardy used to write *Tess of the d'Urbervilles* and *Jude the Obscure* (above). Many of Hardy's possessions were gifted by his second wife, Florence.

Founded in 1846, the Dorset County Museum moved to a purpose-built, Gothic-style building on Dorchester's High West Street in 1881. The founders wanted to represent the cultural and historical heritage of the county and amassed a significant collection over the following decades, including the Thomas Hardy bequest in 1937. The museum closed for major refurbishment in in 2018 and has since re-opened its doors following a £16.4m transformation. Now called the Dorset Museum, there are an estimated four million objects in the collection including important Roman mosaics *(bottom right)*, Jurassic Coast fossils and sculptures by Elisabeth Frink *(top left)*, who had a studio in the county from the 1970s until her death in 1993.   *Right:* Victorian Hall. *Top right:* TASTE Café. *Bottom left: Dorset Quarrymen, Three Workers* by Alfred Palmer.

The Keep Military Museum *(left & top)* sits at the centre of Dorchester in a building that was originally the gatehouse to the Depot Barracks for the Dorsetshire Regiment. It was also the County Armoury. Designed to look like a Norman Castle, it was completed in 1879 and is now a museum that focuses the history of the regiment, particularly in the two World Wars and the Boer War.

*Above: The Charge of the Dorset Yeomanry against the Senussi at Agagia in Egypt on February 26th 1916, by Lady Butler.*

MARY ANNING
"The most eminent female fossilist"

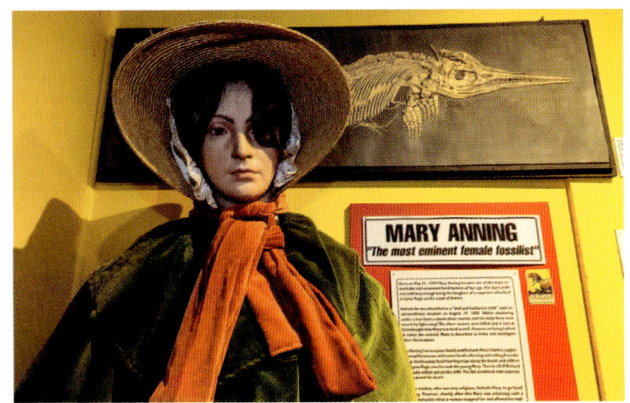

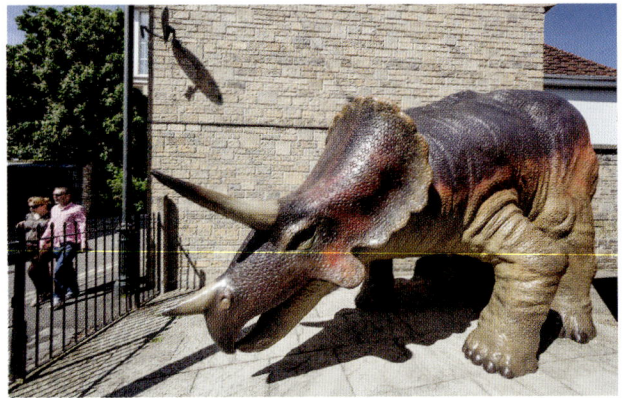

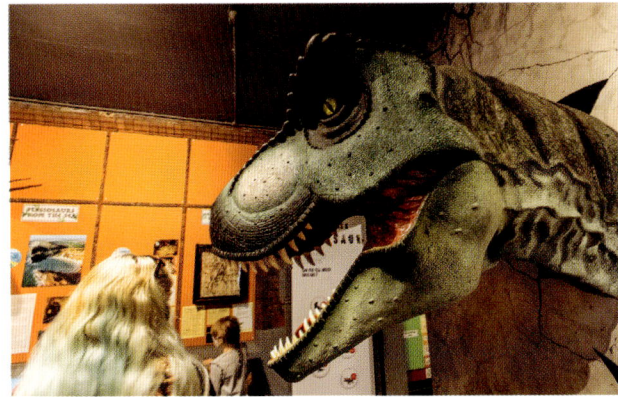

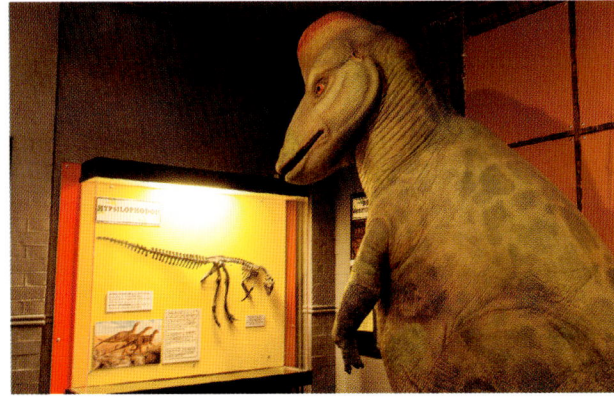

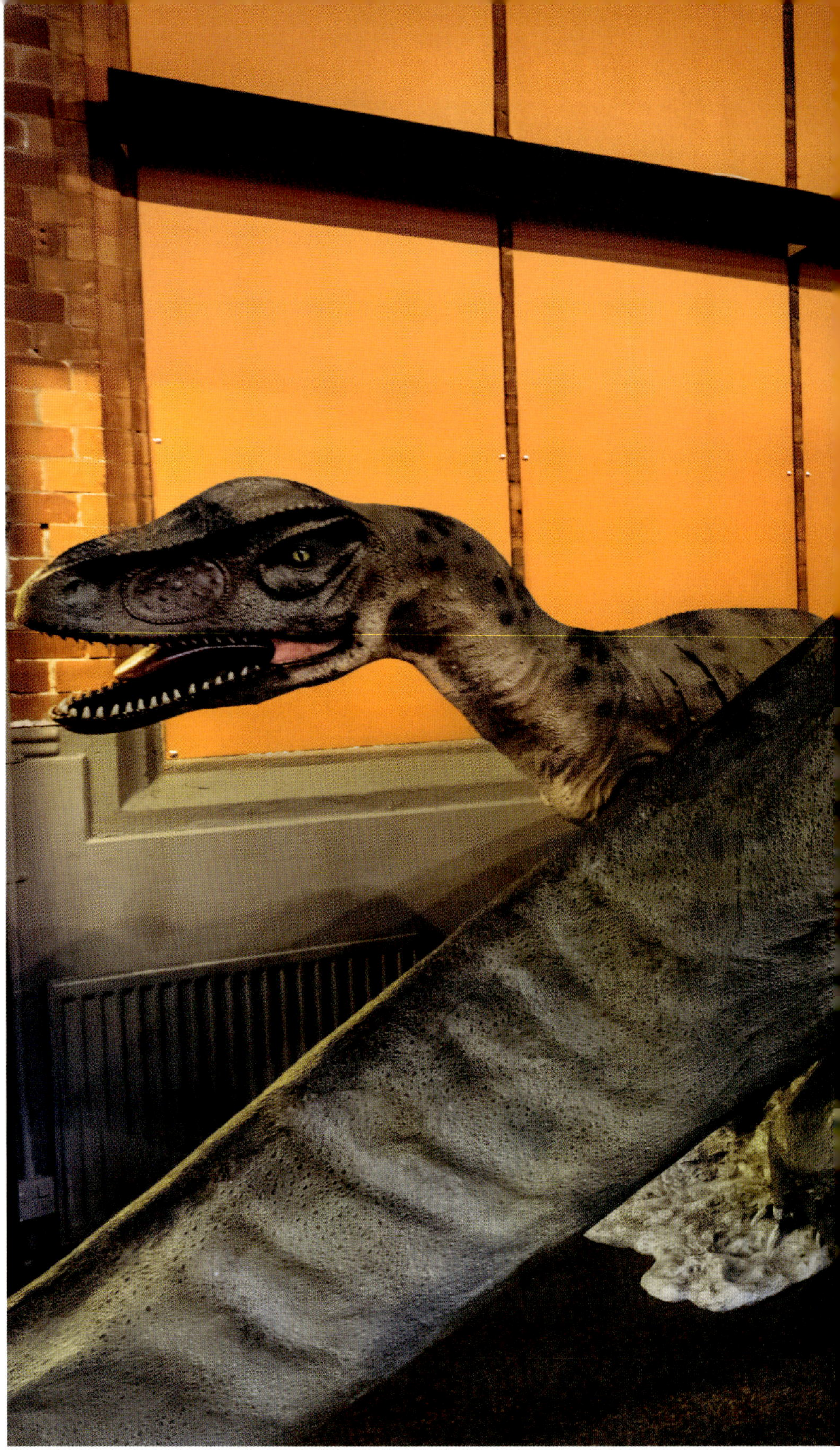

Fossils and dinosaurs are tightly linked to the county of Dorset and the Jurassic Coast; it is hard to travel far without bumping into the odd Tyrannosaurus Rex or two. The Dinosaur Museum in Dorchester has a particular accolade, being the first and only museum to be devoted solely to dinosaurs in mainland Britain. Opened in 1984, the museum is based in a converted Victorian school house and offers interactive displays that take visitors back to the sights, sounds and smells of the time when dinosaurs roamed the earth.

There are a total of seven museums in Dorchester and the range of subjects covered is both fascinating and eclectic. The charming Dorset Teddy Bear Museum *(above)* is a particular favourite with families. The bears on display span more than one hundred years and range from the earliest antique bears to today's bear celebrities known for their appearances in film and on television. Sharing the same building is the Terracotta Warriors Museum *(far right & top right)*. The original clay warriors were created for the First Emperor of China, Qin Shi Hunang di, and a life-sized army of more than eight thousand guarded his tomb. The small group of warriors in Dorchester have been carefully recreated by skilled craftsmen and specialists and are displayed alongside costumed replicas of the First Emperor. The seventh museum, based in an old church on Dorchester's High Street West, is the Tutankhamun Exhibition. The display includes an impressive recreation of the young pharaoh's tomb and associated treasures, including the Golden Mask *(right)*.

On the western edge of Dorchester is Poundbury, an ongoing urban extension that is being specifically built on the planning principles and architectural styles supported by King Charles III. Poundbury is built on Duchy of Cornwall land and the King has been involved with the project since its inception. Construction began in 1993 and more than 4,500 people live here at present, with further plans still in progress.

A statue of Queen Elizabeth, the Queen Mother *(above)* stands in Queen Mother Square *(right)* at the centre of the development and some of the surrounding buildings are named after racehorses that she owned. The Duchess of Cornwall Inn was named in honour of Queen Camilla before she was crowned.

Before heading south to the coast, a worthwhile detour from Dorchester leads north to the Cerne Abbas Giant *(left)*, the largest chalk hill figure in Britain. Standing 55 metres high, the giant is known for his obvious masculinity, which at 11 metres long is a notable fifth of the total. Recent scientific investigations by National Trust archaeologists have suggested that the first construction of the figure is likely to have been in the late Saxon period. The giant is re-chalked every ten years or so to keep it looking white but had to be covered during World War II to prevent its use as a guide for enemy aircraft.

To the south and less than a mile from the sea, is the Osmington White Horse *(above)*. This limestone figure was cut into Osmington Hill, on the South Dorset Ridgeway, in 1808. The rider is a representation of King George III, who had been a regular visitor to nearby Weymouth. It was created as a tribute to the royal visits, but local legend has it that the King was not pleased, as he is depicted riding away from Weymouth rather than towards the town. He did not visit after the figure was in place, but this may well have been due to his declining health.

Weymouth is the largest town in rural Dorset and third only to Bournemouth and Poole in the county as a whole. Although now primarily a resort, Weymouth has a working harbour *(right & above)* and a commercial fishing fleet, as well as boats offering pleasure trips along the Jurassic Coast and to the Isle of Portland. The Town Bridge *(above middle)*, which is more than 90 years old, was built to lift occasionally, allowing larger vessels into the inner harbour. It is now scheduled to lift every two hours. Between 2005 and 2006, a record number of vessels passed under the bridge's leaves – a massive total of 11,528.

Weymouth sits on a sheltered bay at the mouth of the River Wey. It was originally formed of two settlements, Weymouth and Melcombe Regis, which were on opposite sides of the harbour. Elizabeth I united the two towns by Act of Parliament in 1571. One of the sunniest places in England, Weymouth has a temperate climate with milder winters than most of the country.

*Left & above:* Harbourside refreshment and sustenance.

Where the King went, others followed, and the patronage of King George III was instrumental in the development of Weymouth as a tourist destination. The King, together with Queen Charlotte and some of his daughters, first visited in 1789 and were greeted enthusiastically. His doctors had recommended the benefits of sea bathing and the visit was a big success, with the King's health appearing to improve. Regular visits ensued, only ending in 1805 when his health worsened. A statue of the King *(above)* was unveiled on the Esplanade in 1810 as a lasting tribute to this Royal support. It was later painted in the heraldic colours seen today.

Also on the Esplanade is the Jubilee Clock Tower *(right)*, which dates from 1888 and commemorates the Golden Jubilee of Queen Victoria in 1887. Made of iron, the tower has been brightly painted since the 1920s. In recent years, the clock faces have been lit in colours on certain days to promote charitable causes and events.

On the eastern edge of Weymouth and jutting out into the bay is Nothe Fort *(right & above)*, which sits on a peninsula of the same name. It was built to protect the naval harbour at Portland and dates from the second half of the 19th century. Decommissioned in 1956, it now houses a museum with a collection of exhibits and interactive displays charting its significance to the country's coastal defence. The fort has been voted one of the spookiest locations in the UK and modern-day ghost hunters can arrange to visit the atmospheric parapets and passageways, assisted by guides equipped with specialist detecting aids.

The road heading south from Weymouth leads to the Isle of Portland. This tied island is joined to the mainland by Chesil Beach *(right)*, an impressive shingle structure that runs for 18 miles and is one of the best examples of a barrier beach in the world. Although only 4 miles long by 1.5 miles wide at maximum breadth, Portland has a unique character and stunning coastal scenery. There are eight settlements on the island, of which Fortuneswell *(top & right)* is the largest. All are designated as conservation areas. There are a number of listed buildings, including the Grade I listed St George's Church *(above)* at Reforne, which dates from the mid-18th century.

During the 1990s, the local council ran a competition to find a design for a new sculpture to stand on the Isle of Portland. They wanted something that paid tribute to the island's past and chose a design by local artist, Joanna Szuwalska called *The Spirit of Portland*. Unveiled in 2000 and carved from Portland stone, it shows a fisherman and quarryman and stands on New Road near the Portland Heights beacon, with views over Fortuneswell and Chesil Beach *(left, top left & top middle)*.

More sculptures are on display at the Tout Quarry Sculpture Park and Nature Reserve. Worked commercially during the 18th and 19th centuries, the quarry ceased production in 1982 and became a sculpture park, which runs workshops and events relating to all aspects of stone carving. There are many sculptures displayed within the quarry *(top right and above)* and it is often possible to watch stonemasons at work on a new creation. The bare rock faces of the quarry were left for plant and animal life to re-establish themselves naturally. The results include many uncommon plants and lichens. One of Dorset's rarest butterflies, the silver-studded blue, has also been seen here.

The southernmost point of both the Isle of Portland and the county of Dorset is Portland Bill. Over the centuries, the coastline has seen many shipwrecks and warning beacons were lit as far back as Roman times. Permission was finally granted for a lighthouse in the reign of George I. The current lighthouse opened in 1906 and the tower is 43 metres tall.

A white stone obelisk *(right)* was built at the tip of the island in 1844 to warn shipping of a low rock shelf that extends into the sea.

Portland Bill lighthouse was automated in 1996 and has recently been modernised. New LED lamps were installed, and the old, rotating optic *(left & bottom)* is now on display at the base of the tower *(right)*. The lighthouse is monitored and controlled remotely by Trinity House from their planning centre in Essex. A visitor centre *(below)* at the site has exhibitions and interactive displays, including an opportunity to experience what a stormy sea journey would be like in the 'Into the Dark' zone.

Leaving the Isle of Portland and heading west, a detour inland leads to the viewpoint of Black Down. On the summit is the Hardy Monument *(above)* but, in this case, it is not the famous writer who is remembered. The monument was built in 1844 to commemorate Vice-Admiral Sir Thomas Masterman Hardy who is most famous for hearing Admiral Nelson's last words on the deck of HMS Victory at the Battle of Trafalgar. The National Trust have maintained the monument since it passed into their care in 1938. It stands above the village of Portesham where Hardy had his estate and there are lovely views across the surrounding countryside throughout the seasons *(left)*.

At the west end of Chesil Beach is the Abbotsbury Swannery, home to more than 600 magnificent mute swans. It is thought to have been established by Benedictine monks, who lived in a monastery on the site from the 11th century. They would have bred swans to provide food for their banquets. The monastery was dissolved by Henry VIII in 1539 and largely destroyed, although some ruins can still be seen, but the swannery continued. The 25-acre site is now the only place in the world where you can walk through a colony of mute swans while they are nesting. The swans are completely free-flying and do not have to stay here but the protected habitat of the Fleet lagoon, which is sheltered by Chesil Beach, provides an attractive environment.

The area around Abbotsbury, including the village itself and the swannery, is all owned by the Ilchester Estate. The village *(right)* sits in a sheltered valley and so enjoys a warmer micro-climate. St Nicholas' Church *(top)* was built around 1400 as the Parish Church of Abbotsbury. The oldest parts of the building are the tower and north wall. Within the church are more than sixty unique kneelers *(above)*, made by local people and showing many aspects of community life. Abbotsbury is also known for its sub-tropical gardens, which date from the 18th century and are home to many rare plants, including fine displays of magnolia and camellia.

*pp.172-173:* St Catherine's Chapel, built by the monks of Abbotsbury Abbey in the 14th century. Within the chapel are 'wishing holes' where women would pray to St Catherine in the hope that she would find them a husband.

# A JURASSIC JAUNT

Many counties of England are renowned for the wide range of interesting and delicious produce that is grown, reared or made within their boundaries, and Dorset is certainly no exception.

Moores Biscuits has been making bakery goods in the Bridport area for over 140 years. The company moved from its original home in the village of Morcombelake into the centre of town in 2006 and is still owned and run by the Moores family.

Their most famous biscuit is one of Dorset's best-known traditional foods, the Dorset Knob. In the 19th century, these were made from leftover bread dough that was dried out in the ovens, but they are now made from a traditionally fermented dough and given three separate bakes. Their unique texture goes perfectly with cheese, such as Dorset Blue Vinney, a hard crumbly blue cheese that is also made in the county. They are named after a type of hand-sewn button, which originated in Dorset and was popular in the years before mechanisation.

It is no surprise that Bridport has become known as a centre for fine local produce as it is also home to Palmer's Brewery, which is based in a historic building beside the River Brit. The company has been brewing ales here since 1794 and recently celebrated 225 years of continuous operation.

A few miles east of Bridport is Sea Spring Seeds, a specialist plant nursery that is the home of the Dorset Naga, one of the hottest chillis in the world. This was developed from a Bangladeshi chilli but has since been recognised as a distinct variety. It belongs to a group of chillies known as the 'superhots' and averages more than a million Scoville Heat Units, with a maximum of 1.6 million; Jalapeños usually reach a maximum of 8000.

Bridport sits inland but is only a vigorous stone's throw from the sea. The marine landscape along this section of Dorset's Jurassic Coast is very different to that further east and equally as fascinating. The dramatic, crumbly cliffs are tinged with gold at West Bay and our route continues from here to the town of Lyme Regis. On a sunny day, it is hard to imagine that dinosaurs walked here around 190 million years ago, but evidence of their existence is all around.

In the 18th and 19th centuries, Lyme Regis became a very fashionable resort, primarily due to the rise in popularity of sea bathing. The town quickly reinvented itself as a 'watering place' and had a bathing house by 1755.

A philanthropist called Robert Hollis built the first promenade and then established the Assembly Rooms, which helped to draw many important people to the town. Jane Austen visited on two occasions and gained inspiration for her later work.

Two centuries later, Lyme Regis still relies on tourism for its health and prosperity. The resident population is less than four thousand but the town welcomes around 80 thousand overnight visitors and half a million day-trippers a year.

The historic market town of Bridport has Saxon origins and was one of the four most important towns in the county during the reign of King Alfred. Since the Middle Ages, it has been known as a centre for rope and net making; its particularly broad main street was used to dry the ropes. Now it champions the wide range and high quality of local produce and hosts regular street markets twice a week *(above)*, on Wednesdays and Saturdays, as well as popular Farmers' and Vintage Markets that attract visitors from miles around. The town also offers a variety of independent retailers including R.J Balson & Son, a butcher's shop that has been in the same family for more than 500 years *(right)*.

Bucky Doo Square *(left)* sits at the centre of Bridport and there are mixed opinions on the origin of its unusual name. Possible theories link it to The Buck and Doe inn, which may have been located here in the 17th century, or to an Oxford prison called the Bocardo, which had connections with the town. Whatever the reason for the name, it is a good place to sit and admire the mix of buildings. Notable 18th century examples include the Town Hall *(below right)*, which was designed by William Tyler and dates from the 1780s. An interesting carved seat *(above)*, added to the Square in 1976, was created by stonemason Karl Dixon. Regular sessions by musicians and brass bands *(below left)* make this an ideal spot to meet with friends.

Each September, Bridport is transformed with a whirl of colour and creativity. The annual Hat Festival is held at the end of summer and attracts large crowds of people keen to join in the fun. Running over several days, this celebration of wacky headwear centres on Bucky Doo Square and includes music and competitions. From racecourses and fish to carousels and clocks; if you can add it to a hat, you can see it at the Bridport Hat Festival. The main event happens on a Saturday, or 'Haturday' as it is known. As the popular saying goes, 'If you want to get ahead, get a hat'.

Just over a mile from Bridport is the small settlement and stunning coastline of West Bay. Part of Dorset's Jurassic Coast, the dramatic East Cliff dominates the beach below and rises to a height of 43 metres above sea level. Mainly formed of Bridport Sand, the crumbly texture of the cliff makes it very susceptible to erosion and rockfalls. Although the area has been used by film crews for many years, it has become increasingly popular with visitors since being a main location for the ITV drama *Broadchurch*. The famous introductory sequence of the BBC series *The Fall and Rise of Reginald Perrin,* where the lead character abandons his clothes on the beach before swimming out to sea, was also filmed here.

The settlement of West Bay sits on the coast, between the East and West Cliffs, at the mouth of the River Brit, and was originally called Bridport Harbour. The current harbour *(right)* has changed position twice over the centuries and was initially further inland nearer to Bridport town. The harbour was historically used to export the ropes and nets made locally but is now mainly frequented by fishing boats and tourists. The Customs House Emporium on the edge of the beach is a Grade II listed, former boat shed that is now home to a café and many small stalls offering a range of quirky treasures *(above left & right)*.

Just to the west of Bridport, Colmer's Hill *(right)* rises to a height of 417 feet above the village of Symondsbury and is part of the Symondsbury Estate. A gentle stroll to the top of this distinctive, cone-shaped hill takes about forty-five minutes and offers stunning views over the surrounding countryside. The Estate covers over 1500 acres of beautiful Dorset landscape and is privately owned but offers a wide range of facilities and opportunities for visitors. Manor Yard is at its centre and has a variety of specialist shops including the Home & Garden Store *(above middle)* and the Sou'-Sou'-West Gallery with work by artists including Brendon Murless *(above)*.

*Top:* Church of St John the Baptist, Symondsbury.

Another popular attraction on the Symondsbury Estate is the collection of farm animals that live in the paddocks above the car park. Full of character, they all have names and individual personalities. The donkeys, Gretel and Florence *(left and above left)*, have been in residence since 2019 and there are also rare breed Oxford Sandy & Black sows *(top right & above right)*, pygmy goats *(top left)*, sheep and chickens.

Ten miles west of Bridport is the attractive seaside resort of Lyme Regis, home to a harbour wall that features in both film and literature. Called the Cobb, this wall has a key role in both Jane Austen's *Persuasion* and *The French Lieutenant's Woman* by John Fowles. Built to protect the town and ships from the sea, the Cobb is a perfect place for a stroll when weather conditions are fair but special care may be needed when attempting the steps that link the upper and lower levels, as it is from these that Louisa Musgrove tripped and fell in Jane Austen's novel – although all turns out well by the final chapter.

Known as the 'Pearl of Dorset', Lyme Regis is a popular destination for holiday makers who come to enjoy the beautiful scenery found at this section of the Jurassic Coast. Built at the mouth of the River Lym, the town sits between the Undercliffs National Nature Reserve to the west and the Blue Lias cliffs to the east. Lyme was mentioned in the Domesday Book and received its first Royal Charter from Edward I in 1284, at which point it became Lyme Regis. A range of events are held throughout the year, including the annual Fossil Festival each April.   *pp.192-193:* Views of Lyme Regis.

One of Lyme Regis' most famous residents was Mary Anning, who was born here at the end of the 18th century. She became a world-renowned palaeontologist, fossil collector and dealer, finding her specimens in the local cliffs. The Lyme Regis Museum *(p.194 bottom right)* now stands on the site of her house and the film *Ammonite,* starring Kate Winslet, was inspired by her life. The Guildhall *(p.194 top)* stands next to the Museum on Bridge Street and is still used for town council meetings, community events and weddings. It is a Grade II* listed building and dates from the late 19th century, although there has been a guildhall in the town since Elizabethan times. Italianate in style, it was designed by George Vialls. *Above & p.194 bottom left:* Lyme Regis seafront.

The geology of Lyme Regis is amongst the most interesting on earth and fossils found locally have changed the way that scientists interpret prehistoric life. As well as holding an annual Fossil Festival, the town is home to the Dinosaurland Fossil Museum, which is based in an old church and has over 16,000 exhibits, including a large collection of Ichthyosaurs and Ammonites. The church is a Grade I listed building and it was here that Mary Anning was baptised in 1799.

One of the most popular and interesting activities to try at Lyme Regis is fossil hunting. To find something that was living millions of years ago, and to hold it in your hand, appeals greatly to the human sense of curiosity. The beaches between Lyme Regis and Charmouth are good places to start, and winter is the best season to visit as erosion levels are higher and there are fewer people around. It is always important to check tide levels before starting, both for safety reasons and to improve the chance of success. Fossils are revealed as the tide recedes, so this is the best time to go. Guided tours led by fossil experts are available locally.

Although many of the boats that use Lyme Regis harbour are pleasure craft, there is still a small but successful fleet that fishes in the waters of Lyme Bay. Fishing was originally the main activity in the town, with the 19th century being the peak time for the industry. During World War II, boats were commandeered for use by the Royal Navy, with only two boats left for fishing. There are currently around a dozen boats that use Lyme harbour as their base. Parts of the Bay were closed to bottom-towed fishing in 2008 in an attempt to protect the reefs and improve the long-term conservation of the habitat that includes one of the largest colonies of pink sea fans in Britain.

# FAR FROM THE MADDING CROWD

Although it is hard to leave the dramatic Jurassic Coast behind, the rural interior of Dorset does not disappoint and our journey across the landscape from west to east includes ancient abbeys, imposing stately homes and a particularly recognisable street.

Covering an area of just over 1000 square miles, Dorset is predominantly rural, and the unique geology of the county is just as important inland as on the coast. More than half of the total area has been designated as an Area of Outstanding Natural Beauty, the fifth largest in the country.

Chalk downlands, limestone ridges and low-lying clay valleys provide varied habitats that are perfect for flora and fauna; more than 80% of Britain's mammal, bird and butterfly species can be found here.

There are very low levels of light pollution in rural Dorset. In particular, the AONB of Cranborne Chase has been designated as an International Dark Sky Reserve. Dark night skies are not only loved by astronomers but also by wildlife, attracting species including brown hares, otters and goshawks.

As well as providing inspiration for Thomas Hardy, rural Dorset has also been appreciated and represented by a variety of artists and musicians over the centuries. In 1816, John Fisher became the vicar of Gillingham, near Shaftesbury. He was a close friend of the artist, John Constable who came down to visit in the 1820s and produced paintings of the area, including one of the local mill.

The Dorset landscape also held great appeal for artist, Paul Nash. He created more than 80 artworks of the county between the mid-1930s and his death in 1946, with subjects including the Iron Age hillforts of Maiden Castle and Badbury Rings.

A visit to Dorset was also behind music composed by Gustav Holst. Although partly of Swedish descent, Holst was born in the town of Cheltenham. He enjoyed going on walking tours in the Dorset countryside and had been an admirer of Thomas Hardy for many years. Inspired by the first chapter of Hardy's novel *Return of the Native,* he began working on a composition called *Egdon Heath*. Holst met and talked with the great writer in the 1920s and dedicated the piece to him. The premier took place in London just a month after Hardy's death in 1928 and Holst considered it amongst his finest work.

The Dorset countryside is dotted with quirkily named hamlets and villages. From Affpuddle and Minterne Magna to Purse Caundle and Sixpenny Handley, there is plenty of scope for aficionados of Douglas Adams' much-loved book, *The Meaning of Liff*.

Since 2008, Dorset has had its own county flag. A public competition was held, and the winning design has a white cross, with a red border on a gold background. This was particularly suitable, as all three colours also appear in the coat of arms of Dorset County Council. The golden background is said to represent the sandy beaches and also the well-known landmarks of Golden Cap and Gold Hill.

Heading inland from Lyme Regis, the verdant Dorset countryside is much loved by walkers, cyclists and other outdoor enthusiasts. Lambert's Castle is an Iron Age hillfort found to the north of the village of Fishpond Bottom and a walk to the top offers rewarding views over Marshwood Vale *(left)*. Rising to a height of 256 metres, the fort dates back 2,500 years and is a Site of Special Scientific Interest. A second fort, Coney's Castle, is a mile or so to the south. Four miles to the east, there is another good viewpoint at Pilsdon Pen *(below)*. This hillfort is the second highest point in Dorset at 277 metres, being topped only by Lewesdon Hill, which is just to the east and a mere two metres higher. All the forts are cared for by the National Trust.

On the north-west corner of Dorset's boundary is the graceful building of Forde Abbey, a former Cistercian monastery that is now privately owned. The house and grounds both open to the public and the award-winning gardens are home to a fountain that reaches a height of almost 50 metres. The abbey dates from the 12th century and was surrendered peacefully during the dissolution of the monasteries some 400 years later. The working area of the original building, including part of the cloisters, the monk's sleeping accommodation, kitchens and refectories are still part of the current house, as is the chapter house. Popular as a filming location, the abbey was used as a key location in the 2015 film of Thomas Hardy's *Far from the Madding Crowd* starring Carey Mulligan.

A Grade I listed building, Forde Abbey is home to an important collection of beautiful Mortlake Tapestries. These were worked from cartoons by Raphael, which are now in the collection at the V&A. Five of the seven original cartoons can be seen as tapestries at the Abbey and they have hung here for around 300 years. They were made by the Mortlake Tapestry Works in the first half of the 17th century. As well as being open to the public from March to October, Forde Abbey also hosts weddings and events.

*pp.208-209:* Interior views with Mortlake Tapestries *(p.209 middle right),* Cloisters *(p.209 bottom left)* and Gift Shop *(p.209 bottom middle).*

There are many important historic buildings in Dorset and just east of the town of Beaminster is another notable example; the manor house of Mapperton *(right & above middle)*. Although privately owned, the house sits in award-winning grounds *(top)* that open regularly during the season. Guided tours of the interior are also offered on certain days. The estate was listed in the Domesday Book of 1086 and then passed through the hands of only four families until the early 20th century. It is currently the home of family members of the Earl of Sandwich. Paintings in the Mapperton collection include works by William Hogarth, Sir Peter Lely and Sir Joshua Reynolds. Percy, a much-loved African spurred tortoise *(above)* enjoys a heated home within the grounds.

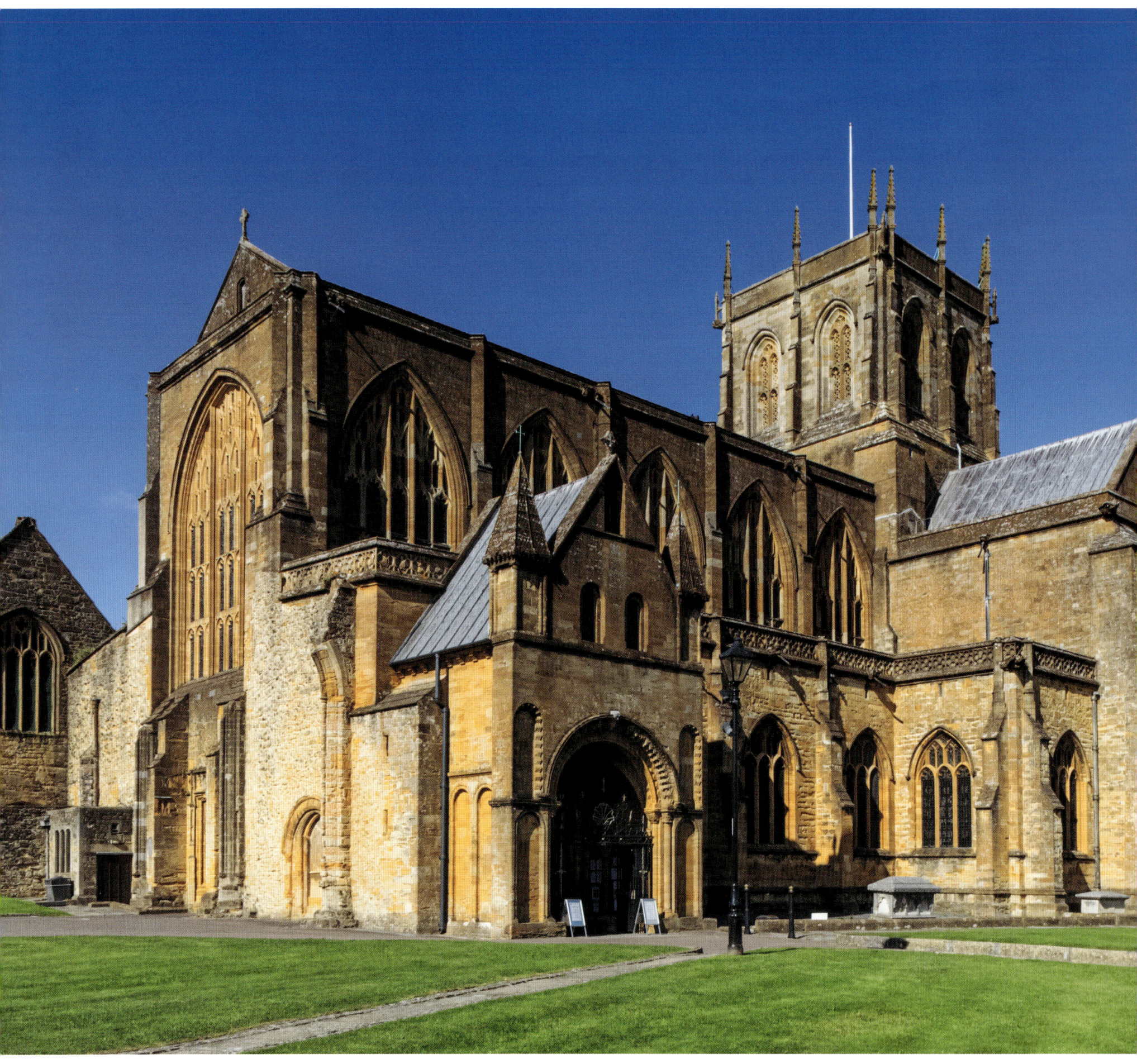

Following Dorset's northern border eastwards leads to the town of Sherborne and the historic Sherborne Abbey *(left)*. Founded in the 8th century as a Saxon cathedral, it was later the abbey church for a Benedictine Monastery prior to becoming a parish church in the reign of Henry VIII. Known by many as the 'cathedral of Dorset', it is the burial site of two Saxon Kings and was a place of worship for Sir Walter Raleigh. Also called the Abbey Church of St Mary the Virgin, its bells are said to be the heaviest peal of eight in the world. During the 15th century, Sherborne Abbey was substantially rebuilt and the beautiful fan vaulting in the nave was finished towards the end of this period.

*Above (clockwise from top left):* Fan vaulting; Exterior view; West Window installed in 1997 (designed & created by John Hayward); Organ; The Digby Memorial.

The Great East Window in Sherborne Abbey sits at the end of the Quire (right) and was designed by the prestigious Victorian firm of Clayton and Bell. Installed in 1858, it features the four Apostles and other biblical subjects. Below the window is the altar, backed by a reredos (top) also dating from the mid-19th century with figures carved in Caen stone by James Forsyth. Contemporary reports noted the cost of the reredos as £565, equivalent to nearly £90,000 today. There are a number of fine tombs within the abbey, including the 16th century Leweston tomb in St Katherine's Chapel (above).

Sherborne Old Castle *(above left & right)* dates from the 12th century and was originally a fortified palace for the Bishop of Salisbury. A Royalist stronghold in the Civil War, the castle was finally overcome by Parliamentary forces in 1645 and was badly damaged. At the end of the 16th century, Sir Walter Raleigh fell in love with the estate and was granted the lease by Elizabeth I. He had a lodge built to accommodate his visits. Now cared for by English Heritage, the old castle sits within the grounds of Sherborne Castle and opens to visitors between April and October.

Sherborne Castle *(above & p.216 top right)*, also known as Sherborne New Castle, grew up around the lodge originally built by Sir Walter Raleigh in the Tudor period. The diplomat, Sir John Digby acquired the estate in 1617 and it has now been in the Wingfield Digby family for over 400 years. The castle was used as headquarters for commandos involved in the D-Day landings of World War II. It is home to important collections of art, porcelain and furniture and can be visited on certain days. The two castles are separated by a lake created by Capability Brown in the middle of the 18th century, and both grounds open regularly in the tourist season.

Still in the rural north of Dorset is the town of Shaftesbury, home of a very famous street. Instantly recognisable to those of a certain age, the ancient cobbles of Gold Hill *(left)* appeared in an advert from the 1970s for Hovis bread that still regularly features in programmes looking back at the most memorable commercials of all time. Directed by Ridley Scott, the advert was later parodied in a sketch by The Two Ronnies.
A recent painting *(above)* looking to the top of the hill, by locally-based artist Janet Swiss, visualises a busy market day in the time before the Town Hall was built in 1827.

In the 9th century, King Alfred the Great founded an abbey in Shaftesbury that was the first religious house solely for women *(above middle)*. His second daughter was the first Abbess and the community flourished for centuries until becoming the last abbey destroyed by Henry VIII in 1539. Little of the structure remains but a museum displays findings from the site *(above left & right)* and also has a digital display showing how the abbey may have looked at the height of its power. The gardens of the Shaftesbury Abbey Museum surround the excavated foundations of the original building and offer a peaceful place to visit. Created by Rupert Moore, a stained-glass roundel *(right)* in the shrine to St Edward commemorates King Edward the Martyr, who was murdered at Corfe Castle in the 10th century. His body was later brought to the Abbey and remained there until after the Reformation.

*Top left:* Shaftesbury Town Hall.  *Top right*: One of a series of four murals within the Town Hall, by Phyllis Wolff, depicting the history of Shaftesbury Abbey.

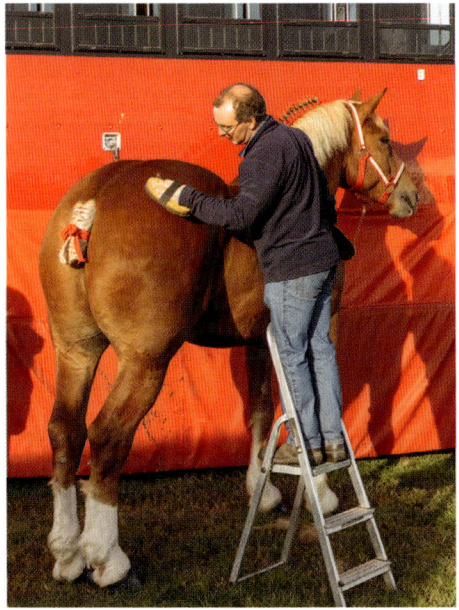

The Wessex Heavy Horse Show & Country Fayre started as a show and auction at the Shaftesbury Livestock Market before moving to the Turnpike Showground, just three miles out of town, nearly twenty years ago. A mecca for owners and admirers of all heavy horse breeds, the show attracts up to fifty horses on show day, with a variety of classes to celebrate their characters and abilities.

The small market town of Blandford Forum *(right)* grew up around a fording point of the River Stour and is important architecturally, with many fine buildings dating from the Georgian period. The town was largely destroyed by a massive fire in 1731, with only a few buildings left standing. Funds, including a substantial donation from King George II, were gathered from around the country, allowing the town to be rebuilt over the following decade. The Town Hall *(top right & bottom left)* dates from this period, opening in 1734. Designed by local architects, the Bastard brothers, it is made of Portland Stone and those with 20/20 vision may see the occasional fossil naturally embedded in the façade. The new town layout enabled many improvements to be made and still largely survives today.

*Top left & bottom right:* The Crown Hotel & The Greyhound, both offering beers from Blandford-based brewery, Hall & Woodhouse.

Just to the north-east of Blandford Forum is Blandford Camp, a military base that is home to the Royals Signals and also the location of their museum. The Royal Signals Museum looks at the history of communications within the British Army and explores the enormous developments that have taken place over the last 150 years. A variety of displays and exhibits looks at the challenges presented by the cyber warfare of today as well as exploring the past, when the introduction of the telegraph was seen as a great advance. The museum has been at Blandford since 1997 but was founded nearly 100 years ago.

A regular feature of the county's events calendar is the Great Dorset Steam Fair, which takes place over the August bank holiday weekend. This massive heritage event celebrates Britain's industrial and agricultural past in spectacular style. The fair began in 1969 and moved to its current location at Tarrant Hinton nineteen years later. The 600-acre site now attracts up to 200,000 people over five days. Steam exhibitions and demonstrations are central to the event, with more than sixty showman's engines *(right)* travelling long distances to take part.

*Top:* Fairground helter-skelter.

*Above:* Interior of traditional Romany caravan.

The magnificent display of fairground organs is a major attraction at the Great Dorset Steam Fair. These large, intricate instruments each have an individual character created both by their sound and by their unique decoration. Originating in Paris, these organs were designed to be heard above the noise of the fair. The tunes are created by the use of music books; linked pieces of thick cardboard with punched holes that are picked up by the organ's mechanism as they move through.

The atmosphere of the Great Dorset Steam Fair is created, in part, by all the characters and entertainers who enter into the spirit of the occasion. The fairground at the event is world-famous and is one of the largest that travels around Britain. Traditional steam-driven carousels sit alongside modern, adrenaline rides and there are hundreds of side stalls ready to entice the visitor.

The Great Dorset Steam Fair is no stranger to the Guinness Book of Records. A new world record was made in 2013, when a total of 103 steam rollers entered the main arena together, beating the previous record, also made at the show a decade earlier, by 71.

Five years later, at the 50th Anniversary Show, more than 500 steam engines travelled from all over the world, including countries as far-flung as New Zealand and Canada, to achieve the world record for the largest display of steam powered vehicles.

*Also p.202*

The Norman church of Knowlton dates from the 12th century and sits at the centre of a Neolithic henge. This unusual juxtaposition is symbolic of the move from Pagan traditions to Christianity. The church was in use until the 17th century, serving a riverside hamlet that no longer survives. Known as Knowlton Rings, the site is now cared for by English Heritage and is accessible during daylight hours.

*pp.238-239:* Beech avenue at Moor Crichel.

*p.240:* Boscombe.